GHOST HUNTERS OF NEW ENGLAND

Count the typos and grammer errors in this book!

D0971384

GHOST HUNTERS OF NEW ENGLAND

Alan Brown

University Press of New England   *Hanover and London*

Published by University Press of New England,
One Court Street, Lebanon, NH 03766
www.upne.com
© 2008 by University Press of New England
Printed in the United States of America
5 4 3 2 1

All rights reserved. No part of this book may be reproduced in any form or by any electronic or mechanical means, including storage and retrieval systems, without permission in
writing from the publisher, except by a reviewer, who may quote brief passages in a review.
Members of educational institutions and organizations wishing to photocopy any of the
work for classroom use, or authors and publishers who would like to obtain permission for
any of the material in the work, should contact Permissions, University Press of New England, One Court Street, Lebanon, NH 03766.

Library of Congress Cataloging-in-Publication Data

Brown, Alan.
Ghost hunters of New England / Alan Brown.
    p.   cm.
Includes bibliographical references and index.
ISBN 978–1–58465–720–0 (pbk. : alk. paper)
  1. Parapsychology—New England. 2. Parapsychology—
Investigation. 3. Ghosts—New England. I. Title.
BF1028.5.N49B76   2008
133.10974—dc22   2008010983

Contents

Acknowledgments

I would like to thank the directors, co-directors, and members of all of the paranormal research groups that agreed to be included in this book. I am also indebted to those directors who either consented to a second interview or sent me additional information. Finally, I am grateful to Tabitha Denihan for helping locate several groups that were not listed in Shadowlands.

Introduction

Ghost Hunters of New England is the second of my regional books on American paranormal investigating groups. The first was *Ghost Hunters of the South*, which was published by the University Press of Mississippi. I wrote both of these books because of the public's current fascination with ghosts and the people who hunt them. I found out about the groups included in booth books by checking out the Shadowlands search engine, which provides a state-by-state listing of the web sites of American ghost-hunting groups. In both books, the state-by-state approach lends individuality to the various groups, most of which derive a sense of identity from the historical sites they investigate.

In the mind of the general public, two regions in the United States have acquired the reputation of being haunted: the South and New England. In the South, the tragic legacy of slavery and the horrors of the Civil War have combined to create a body of ghost lore that still attracts visitors to the region's charming antebellum homes and its rolling battlefields. One could argue, however, that New England has a better claim as America's most haunted region, owing primarily to its extreme age. However, age alone cannot explain the endurance of the supernatural aura that descended upon New England almost from its very inception.

To the early English settlers, who settled in Plymouth in 1620, Salem in 1628, and Massachusetts Bay in 1630, the New World was a mysterious place indeed, fraught with harsh winters, a rugged landscape, and savage inhabitants.[1] In the writings of William Bradford and Captain John Smith, the reader gets the impression that the Indians must be in league with the devil, owing to their barbaric ways. The witch-hunting fever, which many of the early colonists had brought with them to the New World from England, manifested itself in Salem not very long after it was founded. From June through September 1692, nineteen men and women were taken in carts to a barren slope near Salem Village called

Gallows Hill and hanged. In addition, a man in his eighties named Giles Corey was pressed to death under heavy stones.[2] A minister at Boston's Old North Church, Cotton Mather, was also a self-proclaimed witch hunter whose most famous book, *The Wonders of the Invisible World* (1693), is a classic account of the Salem Witch Trials. In his account of the first witch brought to trial, Bridget Bishop, Mather includes the testimony of William Stacy, who claimed that Bishop's "shape" appeared in his room one night and followed him to the barn, where "he was very suddenly taken or lifted from the ground, and thrown against a stone wall; after that, he was again hoisted up and thrown down a Bank, at the end of his house."[3]

The hysteria that culminated in the Salem Witch Trials dissipated not long after the last witch was hanged, but the incident left an imprint on the region that very quickly manifested itself in folklore. Soon, New England became firmly established as a place where dark forces dwelled. For example, a Quaker Cemetery in Leicester, Massachusetts, called Spider Gates is said to be haunted by disembodied voices and screams, which resonate from the modest little graveyard.[4] In northwest Connecticut near the town of Cornwall, a small village called Dudleytown was completely abandoned in 1899 because of outbreaks of murder, suicide, and madness that had plagued the small community since its founding by Gideon Dudley in 1748.[5] It is said that in Barre, Vermont, a young stonecutter named Joe McIntosh drained the blood of his first wife, turning her into a vampire.[6] In the local cemetery in York, Maine, the husband of a witch, Mary Nasson, placed a large stone slab over her grave to keep her inside.[7] Island Path Road in Hampton Beach, New Hampshire, is haunted by the ghost of Goodwife Cole, who cursed a group of mariners who taunted her. After their ship sank, Cole was fined. Following her death, a stake was driven into her body, which was buried, exhumed, and reburied several times. Sightings on Island Path Road include a figure that appears in the fog, lights that flicker, and objects that move by themselves.[8] In Providence, Rhode Island, the ghost of writer Edgar Allan Poe walks the street where a woman he dated once lived.[9]

Fittingly, New England became the focal point of the spiritualist movement in the United States. In 1852, a Boston woman, Mrs. W. B. Hayden, was one of the first mediums who popularized the notion that it was possible to communicate with the spirit world.[10] That same year, Daniel Douglas Home, a medium from Greenville, Connecticut, astounded spectators by levitating from the floor of the Connecticut home of Ward Cheney during a séance.[11] On October 5, 1861, a Boston engraver and amateur photographer named William Mumler was developing some self-portraits when he was startled to find the image of spectral woman on several of his photographs. Mumler was the first to specialize in what became known as spirit photography.[12] Chittenden, Vermont, earned a reputation among Spiritualists as "the Spirit Capital of the Universe" because of strange events that were transpiring at a farm owned by two middle-aged, illiterate brothers, William and Horatio Eddy. In 1874, an attorney named Colonel Henry Steel Olcott spent ten days on the Eddy farm, hoping to debunk the activity that hundreds of guests to the home had been reporting. After witnessing the appearance of the ghost of a gigantic Native American at the mouth of a cave and a line of spirits that paraded out of a cabinet, Olcott left the farm, convinced that the two brothers could make contact with the dead.[13] In 1885, the American Society for Psychical Research was founded in Boston, Massachusetts, by William Barrett. One of its founding members, pioneering American psychologist William James, determined that the society would use only trained researchers, who would employ the scientific method in their investigations.[14]

Stories and novels written in the nineteenth and twentieth centuries contributed to New England's growing reputation as the place where ghosts and demons reside. Washington Irving's short story "The Devil and Tom Walker" describes an encounter between a hen-pecked husband and the devil himself in an inlet a few miles from Boston. Nathaniel Hawthorne, whose ancestor, John Hawthorne, was a judge during the Salem Witch Trials, created an entire body of fiction based largely on the sinful ways of the Puritans who settled in New England two centuries before. Like Irving, Hawthorne portrayed an encounter with Satan in a woods outside of Boston, in his short story "Young Goodman Brown." Edgar Allan Poe, who was born in Boston, Massachusetts, on January 19, 1809, published his first volume of poetry, *Tamerlane and Other Poems*, in Boston after his father refused to allow him to return to the University of Virginia.[15] Howard Phillips Lovecraft, who was born on August 20, 1890, in Providence, Rhode Island, wrote a number of short horror stories set in his home town, stories such as "The Shuttered Room." Best known as the creator of his own cosmology, "The Cthulu Mythos," Lovecraft achieved in the 1920s and 1930s fame as Poe's successor in the field of horror fiction. Shirley Jackson's popular novel *The Haunting of Hill House* (1959) is set in a Victorian mansion in New England. Stephen King, surely one of the most popular novelists of the twentieth century, has set many of his novels in and around Bangor, Maine. Thanks to two centuries worth of poetry, short stories, and novels, readers the world over are convinced that New England is indeed a very haunted place.

In the twentieth and twenty-first centuries, film and television have certain added to New England's supernatural mystique. Connecticut residents Ed and Lorraine Warren, who founded the New England Society for Psychic Research in 1952 and opened the Occult Museum, stepped into the spotlight after investigation of the Amityville haunting. Following the publication of Jay Anson's best-selling 1977 book *The Amityville Horror* and two film adaptations of the book in 1979 and 2005, as well as a number of television documentaries, the Warrens became national and international celebrities. In 2004, the Sci-Fi Channel premiered *Ghost Hunters*, a half-hour reality show featuring the investigations of The Atlantic Paranormal Society (TAPS), a group of paranormal researchers based in Warwick, Rhode Island. Many of the sites investigated by TAPS are located in New England.

In April 2007, I contacted the directors of each group by e-mail and set up telephone interviews. Each group was asked the same questions during the interviews:

What is your day job?
How did you first get interested in ghost hunting?

When did your group get started?

What is your overriding philosophy or goal?

How many members do you have?

What are the backgrounds of your members?

Do you charge for investigations?

Do you prefer to investigate in the daytime or at night?

Do you prefer historic sites or private residences?

What kinds of equipment do you use?

Does each member buy his or her own equipment?

What is your view of orbs and EVPs [electronic voice phenomena]?

What percentage of your investigations reveal genuine hauntings?

Are you disappointed when you find an alternate or scientific explanation for the disturbances?

Which of your investigations do you feel are most successful in terms of proving the existence of the paranormal?

Can you recall anything that happened during one of your investigations that was particularly memorable?

Have any of your members been visibly frightened during an investigation?

What kinds of criticism or obstacles have you encountered over the years?

Because TAPS did not respond to any of my requests for an interview, I drew the information for their profile from published articles and interviews.

The distribution of paranormal research groups in New England is clearly determined by population. With the exception of Rhode Island, the largest states have the largest numbers of ghost-hunting groups[16]:

STATE	POPULATION	NUMBER OF GROUPS
Massachusetts	6,349,097	9
Connecticut	3,405,565	7
Maine	1,274,923	4
Rhode Island	1,048,319	3
New Hampshire	1,235,786	2
Vermont	608,827	2

Population also seems to determine the number of paranormal research groups in the South. In my book *Ghost Hunters of the South*, the state with the largest number of ghost-hunting groups

(Georgia—eight groups) is the second largest Southern state (population 8,186,453). Although not all of the paranormal research groups in New England agreed to an interview, the majority of the New England groups listed in Shadowlands did talk to me.

I admit that I embarked on this project assuming that New England ghost hunters would be similar to Southern ghost hunters. This assumption proved to be true in that several investigators from both regions view electronic voice phenomena (EVPs) as being more significant than orbs, those translucent spheres that sometimes appear on photographs. Almost all ghost-hunting groups buy their own equipment. Very few charge anything for investigations, with the exception of travel money in a few cases. The missions of New England and Southern groups are twofold, for the most part: to prove the existence of the paranormal, and to help people who are experiencing disturbances in their homes or businesses. Most science-based groups visit a site with the intention of disproving the haunting. Groups from both regions attract members from all walks of life.

However, there are two important differences between paranormal research groups from New England and those from the South. First, more groups from New England include demonologists in their membership, possibly because so many Southern groups live in the Bible Belt, which condemns anything even remotely connected with the demonic. Second, the New England groups, as a whole, not only are fans of the *Ghost Hunters* television show, but also believe that it has made the general public more interested in the field of paranormal research. Southern groups, on the other hand, tend to be much more critical of the show. John Zaffis, the director of the paranormal Research Society of New England, ascribes the Southern groups' disdain for *Ghost Hunters* to the fact that TAPS is based in Rhode Island: "What I think it boils down to is that the South still hasn't gotten over the Civil War."

It is tempting to credit TAPS with creating the image New England now enjoys as the center for paranormal research in the United States. Actually, though, TAPS and all of the other ghost-hunting groups included in this book are building on the lore that has accumulated in New England for over three centuries. They would be the first to say that were it not for the ghost legends and literary works that have been generated in New England, they probably would never have gotten into the field in the first place.

GHOST HUNTERS OF NEW ENGLAND

CONNECTICUT

NEW ENGLAND SOCIETY FOR PSYCHIC RESEARCH

Monroe, Connecticut
Lorraine Warren, Director
www.warens.net

The New England Society for Psychic Research is the oldest and best-known ghost hunting group in New England. Ed Warren, who founded the group with his wife Lorraine, acquired his fascination with the paranormal while growing up in a haunted house. "The house terrified him as a child," Lorraine said. "It seemed like he had to satisfy his curiosity regarding what happened in that house." Ed met Lorraine while working as an usher at the Colonial Theater in Bridgeport, Connecticut, when he was sixteen years old. He enlisted in the U.S. Navy at the age of seventeen and married Lorraine after his ship sank in the North Atlantic. Following World War II, Ed enrolled in Perry Art School. Two years later, Ed bought a car for fifteen dollars, and he and Lorraine traveled around New England, selling their paintings. "Ed and I were both artists," Lorraine said. "We'd go to a place that Ed had heard was haunted, and he would sketch a picture of the house with ghosts coming out of it." Lorraine showed the pictures to the homeowners, and then she and Ed asked them questions about their homes. "Ed just wanted to see if the same things happened to those families that happened to his family," Lorraine said.

Ed's all-consuming desire to learn more about the entities that were haunting his family home and the homes of the people he had talked to led him to found the New England Society for Psychic Research in 1952. In the group's more than half a century of existence, its members have investigated more that 10,000 hauntings and have taken thousands of photographs of ghosts. Over the years, its membership has included police officers, nurses, doctors, college students, and housewives. The group now has between 250 and 300 members in the United States and in other countries as well.

After Ed passed away on Wednesday, August 23, 2006, Lorraine was not sure that she wanted to continue working with the group anymore. However, the importance of the work she and Ed had been doing for over fifty years changed her mind. "Ed's death made international headlines within hours of his death," Lorraine said. That same week, Tony Spera, Lorraine's son-in-law, called her and told her that the BBC wanted to speak to her. She also spoke to a reporter for a local Bridgeport newspaper. The first question he asked Lorraine was, "Are you going to continue the work?" Lorraine pleaded with the reporter not to ask her that question because she had not decided yet. While she talking to the reporter in her kitchen, she glanced over at a photograph of Ed on the refrigerator. "He had on a T-shirt. The T-shirt said, 'No fear. No excuses.' He had all the members wear them. I stared at the picture for a few moments, then I told the reporter, 'Yes, I'm going to continue my husband's legacy. I'm doing it for him.'"

The mission of the New England Society for Paranormal Research has changed somewhat over the years. In the beginning, the group was interested primarily in investigating hauntings. The group employed some electronic equipment, but it also relied on Lorraine's clairvoyant abilities. Then in 1965, Ed and Lorraine were invited to a home that was haunted by the spirit of little girl named Cynthia, who informed the group, through a medium, that she was looking for her mother. Since then, the group has shifted its focus to helping the living and the dead. Ed and Lorraine's religious beliefs played a very important role in this effort. "A lot of our cases have affected us personally because we put our heart and soul into our work," Lorraine says. "We remember the victims. We remember what they went through. The help we give the victims and their families is always God-given. While we are getting photographs and recordings, we are also intertwined in their lives a great deal. You go in, and you evaluate the situation. If we find the necessity for doing photography or things of that nature, we do. But the first and most important thing is discerning in the house and doing the interviews and walking around the house. Always remember that the overall [objective] is that road that will lead to closure in that place. That's the only time that you really feel you have conquered that situation."

Lorraine's sympathy for earthbound spirits was manifested in a chance meeting she had one day when she was shopping at a local supermarket. A clerk recognized her and asked Lorraine if she had heard about a fatal car crash in Old Town. After Lorraine replied that she had, the woman told her about an experience she and her sister had had while driving up to the Foxwoods Casino in Ledyard: "We got there very late at night. We were coming home, and we saw a young man walking down the road, looking around. I was wondering why he was walking around, alone, in such a lonely place. Then we passed some flowers placed on the side of the road, and I realized that this was the young man who was killed in a wreck that week. At that moment, the young man disappeared." On the way home, Lorraine thought about what the woman had told her. "I realized that this must be a spirit who is not accepting his death and passing on," Lorraine said. "I'd like to ask him all kinds of questions, like, 'Have you been taught any kind of religious beliefs?' or 'Are you going to stay here because you don't want to leave?'" At the time of the interview, Lorraine was thinking of trying to find out the young man's name in the local library and having a prayer said for him in church to help him pass on. "Why was this brought to my attention?" Lorraine wondered. "Was it to see what I would do with [this information]? I was thinking about this today."

Lorraine believes that some earthbound spirits are energized by certain people. She gives the example of a family who calls her group to a house they are leasing because they are experiencing paranormal activity. "The family doesn't really want us to help them, though, because they are embarrassed. They leave, and another family moves in. Nothing happens. This shows me that it is really the makeup of people—their state of mind—that attracts the spirits. [The spirits] could also return because they were born there or they trusted somebody in the house." Nonhuman hauntings, on the other hand, are entirely different. She has found that in most houses where a demon has entered the lives of the homeowners, the family is most likely dysfunctional. "There's alcohol abuse, drug abuse, maybe animosity between family members. All of these things in dysfunctional homes energize demonic spirits.

You can suggest that they get professional help, but if they don't, then blessing the house is not going to last." Lorraine can discern whether or not she is in a happy home almost as soon as she walks inside. It has been her experience that most of the happy homes she has visited are also Christian homes. "We know our faith is important to us," Lorraine said. "For that reason, I am proud to say that God is my copilot."

The most demonic haunting Ed and Lorraine ever investigated is also their most famous case: the Amityville haunting. On November 13, 1974, Ronald DeFeo shot his two brothers and his sister at 3:15 A.M. DeFeo, who had had a serious drug problem, claimed that a shadow had accompanied him on his killing spree. In February 1976, the Warrens become two of only a handful of investigators who were allowed inside the Amityville house, at least partially because of Ed's reputation as a religious demonologist. At the time, George and Kay Lutz, who owned the house at the time, were living at Mrs. Lutz's mother's house in Deer Park. The Warrens were accompanied by a professor from Duke University, a news anchorman from Channel 5 news, and the president of the American Society for Psychic Research. Ed began the investigation by walking through the cellar. Because Ed rarely experienced any clairvoyant sensations, he was surprised to see shadows and pinpoints of light. He commanded the shadows to leave and felt himself lifted into the air. Meanwhile, Lorraine, who was frightened from the outset, climbed up the stairs to the second floor, holding the relics of Padre Pio. As she walked through the bedrooms where the murders had been committed, she was overcome with a feeling of horror. She returned downstairs and conducted a séance in an attempt to ask the spirits of the house what had really happened. All of the investigators were in the room. The heart rate of two of the investigators accelerated so rapidly that they had to sit on the floor. At the same time, the director of a psychic research group in New Haven became so sick that she had to leave the house.

The Amityville case made the Warrens internationally famous, but the notoriety turned out to be a mixed blessing. "We have traveled all over the world—to Australia and the United Kingdom—and they all know what the Amityville Horror was. The language barrier didn't matter. But the Amityville case sticks in my mind because it changed our personal lives a great deal," Lorraine said. "Whatever was there followed us to our own home." That night after the investigation, Lorraine was in bed reading a book on Padre Pio when her two dogs began acting strangely. Then Lorraine found that she could not move. At the same time, she heard a very loud noise, which sounded like large sheets of metal being shaken. Somehow, she managed to climb out of bed and walk toward the doorway, where she was shocked to see a large, black mass. Impulsively, she made the sign of the cross and compelled the entity to leave. Seconds later, Ed walked into the room and led her back to bed. For Lorraine, the Amityville case has never really ended: "It's not one of those cases that you can shelve away. I don't think the Amityville case will ever die."

The Amityville case is certainly the Warrens' most sensational investigation, but it is by no means the only memorable one. A good example is a case they worked on in southern Connecticut. A couple of scientists—a husband and wife team—asked the Warrens to investigate the house with them. They were eager to investigate a real haunted house. A couple from New York was renting a house that used to be a funeral home. Their son had cancer, and they had rented the house so they could be closer to him. "It was one of those old-fashioned funeral homes," Lorraine said. "They embalmed the bodies in the basement and raised them back up with two chain hoists. While we were there, we heard the chains clank together. Well, in the middle of the night, the scientists left. One minute they were there; the next minute, they were gone." Apparently, the married scientists had not been in as many intense situations as the Warrens had.

Ed and Lorraine have worked closely with the clergy over the years to bring closure to their clients and to assist them with expelling demons. Even though the Warrens were devout Catholics, they have asked ministers from a variety of faiths to accompany them on their investigations. "You can't go into a Catholic home with a Protestant minister, or you can't go into a Catholic home with a rabbi. You have to respect the religious denomination of the family who lives there," Lorraine says. However, not every clergyman has agreed to work with the Warrens over the years. "I will always remember something Ed said to a priest once," Lorraine said. "Ed asked him, 'Are you a real priest?' The priest said, 'What do you mean?' Ed said, 'Do you believe in the personification of evil? If you don't, then you aren't a real priest.' Ed didn't raise his voice while talking to the priest. He said it respectfully. He knew, though, that this was not the kind of person you could bring along on an investigation."

Because the New England Society for Psychic Research does not charge for its investigations, Ed and Lorraine lived primarily off the revenue garnered from their lectures. "My son-in-law Tony Spera has been lecturing with Ed and me for twenty-five years. He always did the intros, and when Ed became ill six years ago, he began doing the lectures with me, and he is still doing the research for us." After Ed's death, Lorraine was so much in demand as a speaker that she even had to cancel an appearance on *Oprah* because Oprah wanted to interview her on a date when she had already scheduled a lecture at a university.

Lorraine still feels the presence of her husband. She believes that her husband made his presence known to her on April 5, 2007, the day I interviewed her: "My son-in-law was here today, and we got one of the palm crosses for Ed's grave. My daughter said, 'Oh Mom, this wind is so cold, and you were so sick yesterday. Do you want us to go over and put the cross on Dad's grave?' I said, 'That would be wonderful. Would you?' She said, 'Yes.' So they went over there and cleaned up the grave and put the cross there. It was cold, so I decided I would drive over [to the cemetery] so I could see [the cross]. I sat in the car and talked to Ed and prayed for him. I could see the cross. I told him about going to Heather's and visiting Chris. I was telling him all these things about the family. Then I decided to go to the drugstore. When I came out of the drugstore, I pushed the button for the CD that was in the player. One of Ed's favorite songs that he always thought related to us was 'Their Hearts Were Full of Spring.' It had such beautiful meaning to him. He thought that would be a nice thing to have on a gravestone. He said this to Tony. It was not long after Ed was buried. I was making arrangements for Ed's monument and how I wanted

everything on it. Tony said, 'You know what Ed wanted on there—
'Their Hearts Were Full of Spring'? Well, I put that CD on, and
that song came on the CD.' I called Tony and put the cell phone to
the speaker and said, 'Do you hear that, Tony?' He wasn't there,
but I heard him answer the phone. So I phoned him back, and he
said, 'Lorraine, did you just call me?' He said it was a male voice.
He then said, 'That's beautiful, Lorraine, that's really beautiful.' I
heard my daughter say, 'What's beautiful, Tony?' He told her. Then
he said, 'Lorraine, when I picked up the phone, I didn't hear that
song on the CD. I didn't hear anything on the CD. All I heard was
a man's voice that said, "Who is this?" He said there was no hang-
up. There was only dead air. This was very comforting to me."

Ed and Lorraine Warren have done much more than simply found the New England Society for Psychic Research. They
have written nine books, including *The Haunted: The True Story
of One Family's Nightmare*, a book based on their investigation
of the hauntings that occurred in the Pennsylvania home of Jack
and Janet Smurl. The book was turned into a made-for-television
movie. Ed and Lorraine trained several well-known demonologists, including their nephew, John Zaffis. Their Occult Museum
is a collection of artifacts, masks, idols, dolls, and books located
at the Warrens' home in Monroe. Most importantly, Ed and Lorraine Warren helped to bring paranormal investigation into the
mainstream. As John Zaffis puts it, "Ed was a great man, and he
truly was instrumental in bringing the paranormal to the public's
attention." Lorraine Warren hopes that the New England Society
for Psychic Research will be remembered for all of the good it has
done: "I don't want the public to look on us as religious fanat-
ics, because we're not. We're just a group of people who believe in
their faith and God."

SKELETON CREW PARANORMAL RESEARCH SOCIETY

Cheshire, Connecticut
Jim Petrino, Director
www.mrhaunted.com

Although Jim Petrino believes that he was born with an interest in the paranormal, the media undoubtedly influenced him. "When I was young, I watched a TV show called *In Search Of* with Leonard Nimoy. One of the episodes was *In Search of Ghosts*. That was really the first time I said, 'That is what I really want to do.' I remember turning the lights off in the basement and walking around with a flashlight, trying to find a ghost. When I was ten years old, a book by Daniel Cohen came out called *Real Ghosts*. In the book was a picture called the Brown Lady of Raynham Hall. I thought, 'This was the greatest picture I've ever seen in my life. I want to take pictures of ghosts too.' After I saw the picture, that's all I wanted to do."

Jim's career as a paranormal investigator began as he drove out to cemeteries every weekend and took photographs in the hope of capturing evidence. His skills in spirit photography blossomed under the tutelage of Ed and Lorraine Warren. "I started ghost hunting when I was five years old. I started seriously by taking classes with the Warrens. That was fifteen years ago. I worked with them for years. When I started doing cases with the Warrens, my whole purpose was to observe and record," Jim said. "I was the psychic photographer for the group. Ed Warren said I was the best psychic photographer in the world. But eventually, I discovered that I really enjoyed helping people. It changed my way of looking at evidence. Collecting evidence is great, but when you help someone, you change their life forever sometimes, especially if demonic possession is involved."

Jim's first group was called the Hartford Office for Paranormal Exploration. "That lasted a few years," Jim said. "One of the producers from *PrimeTime* had access to our web site. They called us up and got us on *PrimeTime*. For about a year straight, we were helping out with exorcisms all across the country. Every Wednesday evening, we were helping with an exorcism. That got crazy. Because we were on TV, people would call in and say things like, 'We live in Alabama. My daughter is violent. She scratches herself. She talks in different voices.' Then they talked to the person on the phone and set a date for the exorcism. They'd contact a priest, and we'd meet them at the airport and drive them and give them an exorcism and they'd go home. You can't get statistics on something like that. It was hard to follow up on these people because the next Wednesday, we would be helping someone else. I would say about fifty percent of the exorcisms were successful." After the group disbanded, he started his own group. Because Jim works full-time as a forklift driver for Costco Wholesale, he finds it difficult to find time to go out on investigation. Spending time with his children is a priority in Jim's life right now. "I have enough clients," Jim says. "I don't want any more. I've got a three-year-old and a seven-year-old. My wife and I both work at the same place. I'd love to do more investigations, but I don't have the time." At present, the majority of the group's investigations are done only on Friday or Saturday nights.

Most of the group's twelve members are "regular people." His "right-hand man," Rick Clarke, works in a hospital lab in New Hampshire. The team's membership also includes a security guard, a student, and a person who works with Jim at the store. The age of his members ranges from nineteen to forty-five years old. He regrets that the only thing he and the other members have in common is the investigations. "We don't really have time to go out and socialize afterwards because of the kids," Jim says. His members prefer going to private residences instead of what Jim refers to as the "touristy places." Jim says, "I used to enjoy going through abandoned buildings, but not anymore."

Lately, Jim has been trying to counter the reputation that Skeleton Crew Paranormal Research has acquired as a group of demonologists. "I am not primarily a demonologist," Jim maintains. "We got pigeonholed into that category because we had an exorcism story on our web site. *PrimeTime* read it and put it on TV. When they put it on TV, all of these calls [about demonic possession] came to us. We were like a filter between the priest who did the exorcisms and all the people in the country who needed help. That's how that started." Jim prefers to think of himself as a paranormal investigator instead of as a cleanser of possessed houses. "I probably have the largest ghost picture collection you have probably seen in your life. I have about twenty pictures on my web site. I've got one photo that's amazing." Instead of posting his photographs on the Web, where Jim fears they will be stolen, his team holds slide shows twice a year. "We'll rent out a hall and hopefully people come," Jim says. "I have a friend who is a manager for a community for a bunch of homes where they have a gathering area for magicians or singers. Every week, they will have something different. I've done those for, like, the last five years." Jim's favorite form of community outreach is teaching adult education at the local high school: "That's where I get my new investigators, and that's where I have the most fun now. I call the class 'Ghost Hunting.' The average age in the class size is forty. I love these younger kids. You do this for so long, you lose your spark. Some of these young people who are nineteen or twenty kind of renew your interest."

Unlike many groups in New England, Skeleton Crew Paranormal Research Society's members do not have designated roles. "In my group, we don't have any labels or names or titles," Jim says. "I guess I'm the leader. I'll pick and choose ten to twelve people per case. I worked with a lot of large groups, and it's a madhouse going into a home with a dozen people running around the house, and somebody needs room, and you're trying to get voices on tape and something is moving on video. So I try to keep it small—two or three people—especially if it's a private home. That's usually enough for what we're doing." In April 2007, Jim had a case in New Jersey where the person who was being most affected was the eighteen-year-old daughter. Jim selected for work on the case a twenty-year-old female member of his group and another person whom she was comfortable with. "Kids today want to run around graveyards all night, and I can't do that anymore. I don't have the time or energy," Jim says.

Promoting the group in Jim's area is not difficult because he is so well known. "I have people all the time come up to me and say,

'My cousin's brother has something going on at this house. Will you come over and check it out?' Jim feels he does not have to advertise because his group gets a lot of attention through word of mouth. The group's web site helps as well. "The Internet has changed the whole ghost-hunting thing so much," Jim says. "I get questions from all over the country on the Internet. I pretty much cover all the states on my Buddy List."

Jim feels the same way toward what constitutes viable evidence as most New England ghost hunters do. First of all, he hates orbs: "I've taken hundreds of orbs pictures, and if I get a picture with orbs, I throw it out. If you've seen one, you've seen them all. They seem to be prevalent in haunted locations, but as far as I can tell, they are moisture or something else. I have seen kids take pictures in cemeteries in the rain, and they always get orbs. I say, 'Hey, guys, you can't take pictures in the rain.' I like mists or fogs, though. If you get the foggy stuff in the picture, and you can match it up with somebody who actually lived, that's what I like." EVPs, in Jim's opinion, are amazing because voices cannot be faked. He is so fascinated with EVPs that sometimes he records them in his own house. "I have to go to work at five A.M.," Jim says. "Sometimes, I wake up at three in the morning, and I'll come down to the computer and use my voice recorder and just record silence while I'm down there, and I'll get EVPs all the time. The house was built in 1959. Six months after I bought the house, we bumped into one of the owners, and he said, 'Oh, my God! That house has been haunted forever.' Nothing bad or malevolent, though. The last two owners [were frightened all the time.] I don't acknowledge it all [that it's haunted], but six months ago, we were in the bedroom, and my wife woke up and said, 'There's a ghost in the hallway. It just walked past the doorway.' I said, 'What do you mean?' She said, 'I thought it was you.' I'm only five foot six inches. She said it was about six feet tall. We went into the kitchen to see if anything was there. She was screaming the whole time. The kids woke up, and she said, 'We gotta go.' I said, 'We can't tell the kids there's a ghost in the house.'" As pleased as Jim is with the EVPs he has recorded, his ultimate goal is to photograph a full-body apparition, the Brown Lady of Raynham Hall. "I wouldn't say I've reached my goal yet. I've got a ton of faces, but not the full body," Jim says.

Jim's group does not use psychics, but not because he does believe in them: "I think everyone is psychic to a certain extent. I don't like using them in homes because I have been in situations where there have been two or three psychics in a single house, and somebody blurts out, 'It's the spirit of a little boy who's ten years old.' And the owner hears it and the other psychics pick up different things. 'You're wrong! It's a woman who's ninety years old.' So no, I prefer not to use psychics."

However, Jim has no qualms against using clergy: "I'm Catholic, but I'm open to using anyone who will help. I have only used a Catholic priest, but I would use any denomination." Jim's group members always try to find out the religious beliefs of the client before his group does an exorcism, so that he knows what kind of clergy will need to be brought in. The possessed person's beliefs have little to do with the person's behavior during an exorcism, however: "There were four or five Jewish people who didn't believe in Jesus but were spouting out quotes by Jesus. The same thing has happened with people who did not believe in God at all," Jim says.

One of the group's strangest investigations was conducted at a house in Waterbury, Connecticut. Jim said, "We were in a third-floor apartment, and we got a call that some people were sitting on the front steps and would not go inside until we got there. When we arrived, the girls were trembling on the steps, and I thought, 'This must be a genuine good one.' So we went up to the third floor and jiggled the doorknob, and we couldn't get it open. We got it open, and the handle of the exercise bike was wedged under the doorknob. So we set it down and had an interview with the staff. During the meeting, a twenty-year-old girl was crying and pointing hysterically, 'There it is! There it is! Can't you see it?' I said, 'No, we don't see it.' Rick and I said, 'No we don't see it.' She said, 'It's right there. Don't you see it?' We said, 'No, we can't.'" The young woman continued to point at an unseen presence for thirty minutes. At the end of the interview, the group was getting ready to leave when the young woman claimed she saw the ghost walking down the hallway into the bedroom. "I didn't believe her by this time," Jim said. "I left my camera and my video and just walked down the hallway with her. She pointed to a corner of the bedroom and said, 'Don't you see it?' I said, 'Yeah.' There was a full-bodied apparition standing against the wall. I was thinking, 'What do I do now? I don't have my video camera or my still camera. I don't have anything.' I was afraid it would be gone by the time I returned with my camera, so I took two steps forward, and the thing turned to the side. I took one step, and it disappeared before it hit the wall."

Another creepy investigation was held in Sudbury, Massachusetts. "It started out with UFO [unidentified flying object] sightings," Jim said. "This woman was seeing UFOs over her house. The whole neighborhood was seeing them. The cops were going up and down the road following things. Then she started seeing bones in her house, like a pelvic bone floating down the staircase. A three-dimensional orb would be floating around her house all the time. It would come down to her stomach with a cover over it and disappear and go other places. She was getting frustrated because no one could see it but her." In desperation, she appealed to Jim for help. While Jim, the woman, and several members were standing outside her house, she said, "The orb is over here. Now it's over there." The group saw nothing at the time, but when they ran the film back, they saw a purple orb with a blue ring over it. Jim had another strange experience when he was walking along the woods behind the house. "There was this giant boulder on border between her property and her house," Jim said. "I walked by this boulder, and a word just popped out. Later, we found out that her land was where a famous Indian battle took place with the settlers. She had an Indian shaman come over to try to help her because she thought there might be an Indian burial ground next to her house. She said when this man came to her house, they were walking past this big boulder where I said the word, and she told the shaman, 'This investigator came here, and when he walked past the boulder, he said this word.' She said she wrote it down and didn't think anything of it. The shaman said, 'That's amazing. That's the name of the chief who died by this boulder. He said that the way I said it was exactly the way Native Americans would say it.'"

In spite of Jim's avowed aversion to "touristy places," he admits to have conducted an investigation at the Lizzie Borden house in October 2006. "I think this is one of those things that you cross off your list before you die, so I decided to take the tour," Jim said. "We paid just like a regular guest. They have three bedrooms where you can spend the night. They didn't know that we were going to conduct an investigation. It was ten o'clock. Everyone on the tour who was staying over was going to sleep in the living area to see if anything would happen, so I decided to stay up with them. For an hour or so, we were just sitting around. I didn't want to tell them I was a ghost hunter. An hour went by, and nothing happened, of course, so I said, 'Let me get my tape recorder out of the trunk.' The owner came out of her room. She was curious to see what we were doing. I placed the recorder on the counter top. I said, 'We get voices all the time.' Nobody believed me, of course, so I pressed 'Record' on the tape recorder and said, 'Is anybody here?' I picked up a 'hello' and a 'Get out!' I got three or four EVPs in half an hour there." In the basement where Lizzie Borden supposedly threw her dirty clothes and her weapons, Jim took a picture of the wall above a hole in the wall. "You can see a face," Jim says. "It looks like it's ingrained in the wall. And it matches her father's picture exactly."

Jim's members have never been frightened during an investigation, but Jim did experience a tinge of fear during an exorcism. "The show that I did for *PrimeTime* was the first exorcism I ever participated in," Jim said. "We taped it just for ourselves. This girl [who was possessed] was looking at us with just pure hatred. I have never seen that look again in anyone's eyes. The look this girl gave me was the scariest thing I've ever seen in my life." Jim found out later that the girl became very violent as the priest conducted the exorcism. The video footage taken by the group showed the girl breaking out of her restraints. "Toward the end, she slumped her head down, and everything got quiet," Jim said. "Then a little bitty orb or bubble came out of her mouth and floated up to the ceiling. It was at this point that the entity left her." Even though the behavior exhibited during the exorcism was extremely bizarre, Jim was not exactly "blown away" by the video footage: "I have seen this sort of thing so much that I'm desensitized. It was kind of cool, though." Fortunately, the exorcism was a total success.

Jim is known by his e-mail name, "Mr. Haunted," throughout the world. "This is what my friends call me," Jim says. Some of his friends include his clients. "I always follow up on my cases. Some of them become friends. We send Christmas cards. I am still in contact with some of these people after ten years."

COSMIC SOCIETY OF PARANORMAL INVESTIGATION

Ansonia, Connecticut
Donna Kent and Brian Jones, Co-Directors
www.cosmicsociety.com

The paranormal has held a lifelong fascination for Donna Kent: "As a child, I would hear my name called, and it would be when I was home alone from school, and it would sound like my Dad's voice. Something was mimicking my father's voice. To hear a man's voice that sounded like my Dad is the first memory I have." The depiction of ghostly encounters on television programs also fueled Donna's interest in things otherworldly. "I can remember sitting there on the couch with curlers in my hair for church during an episode of *Lassie* where Lassie was in a ghost town. I was four years old. I was hooked. I guess that's what started me." Ironically, in 1996, Donna was featured on one of the television shows that influenced an entire generation of budding paranormal investigators: *Sightings.* "They did a whole segment on spirit photography, and I was on it," Donna said.

Donna founded the Cosmic Society of Paranormal Investigation in 1995. The group now has two hundred members across the United States, although Donna admits that the membership does fluctuate: "Some of the members across the nation can't really participate on site. The have access and things like that. They also read the newsletter." She describes the members of her group as "adventurous, serious people." Donna says that Cosmic Society of Paranormal Investigation has the largest free collection of spirit energy photos on the Internet. As a result, the group has received recognition far beyond the borders of Connecticut. "In addition to several newspaper articles and several television shows, people find us," Donna said. "The local media is very cooperative. One of our members is a disc jockey on one of our most prominent radio stations around here. It started with him interviewing me around Halloween, and then he began attending some of our meetings and functions, and now he is part of our group."

On one of Donna's public appearances, the interviewer got more than he bargained for. "Many years ago, I went to a haunted place called Carousel Gardens with a radio station. A funny thing happened. It was a country station. The disc jockey was a skeptic. He was mocking the ghost and saying things like, 'I don't believe in this stuff.' And, 'You guys are wasting your time.' And I said, 'If we could just snap our fingers and have the ghosts manifest, we would all be wealthy and probably not be sitting in this room right now.'" As the night went on, the disc jockey continued to provoke the spirits more and more. All at once, he said, "If there is a spirit here, I'd like to see something right now." At that moment, a wine glass sitting on a table across the room shattered, and all the shards of broken glass formed a perfect circle on the floor. Then he began yelling, "Hey! How did you do that?" The disc jockey went from total skeptic to totally terrified in just a matter of minutes.

The mission of the group is to help people who are in the middle of a psychic crisis. "I don't think people should have to live in fear in their own home," Donna says. "This is certainly not to say that every ghost or earthbound spirit is malevolent, but I don't know how many times I've gone to a family's home for visit, and I've discovered that they are staying at a home somewhere else because their house is haunted." Although sometimes hauntings have a positive outcome, Donna admits that sometimes the best thing to do is to move out. Brian Jones, who describes himself as Donna's "main assistant, porter, and significant other," adds that the group's mission is also to help the earthbound spirits who are haunting the house. "It's good for both sides," Brian says. Proving the existence of the paranormal is definitely not one of the group's goals. "I don't have to prove my side to the skeptics," Donna says. "I've been there and done that. I've been wined and dined by the skeptics for information, but I won't do that anymore." Donna knows of groups who spend much of their times taking photographs in cemeteries to collect evidence of the existence of the paranormal, but Donna does not do this anymore because, in her words, "I'm not helping anybody." Wanting to prove the existence of the paranormal too badly can even taint an investigation. Brian confesses that it would be wonderful if proof would come out of their investigations, but making that the goal of an investigation can be dangerous: "Too often, we want something too badly when we are doing an investigation. We make things into what we want them to be instead of seeing them for what they are. We have learned not to be too attached to a desired result."

Donna and Brian go into an investigation prepared to eliminate all of the possible physical causes of the activity in the house. "It's very important to be objective, to observe, document, and to determine the cause [of the disturbance]," Brian says, "and if it is unexplainable, it's paranormal. We don't know exactly what the paranormal is, but as we do more and more investigations, we begin to see patterns, and we are better able to document things. We now know where to set up the camera and where to set up the digital voice recorders. We know what to look for, too." Donna has found even if her group has debunked the haunting in a house, some homeowners refuse to except their explanations: "You don't know how many times I've had people with overactive radiators and noisy furnaces and banging cable wires, and [the clients] still insist that they are haunted. I'd have to say that most people are disappointed when we disprove a haunting. They think it's a novelty to have a ghost in their house." Having a working knowledge of abnormal psychology can also be helpful, from Donna's point of view.

This burning desire to live in a haunted house can be traced back to the popularity of the *Ghost Hunters* television show. Donna says, "I think *Ghost Hunters* has brought in a lot of people who might never even have thought about it. In their everyday lives, they haven't even considered supernatural things. Then one night, they sit down and watch *Ghost Hunters* on the Sci-Fi Channel and

become interested." Donna, who knew Jason Hawes and Grant
Wilson long before they became television stars, was featured on
an episode of *Ghost Hunters*. "It was filmed at the Carousel Gardens Restaurant," Donna says. "It's my home away from home.
For the past twelve years, I've held meetings of the Cosmic Society
there. It is quite actively haunted, so I was thrilled when I heard
that they were coming out there." Donna's role on the episode was
to provide the background on the history and hauntings in the
restaurant.

Brian believes that the popularity of all the television shows
dealing with the paranormal has revealed a side of the American
people that has hitherto been ignored: "The popularity of paranormal television shows is evidence that way more people believe in
the paranormal than not, even in today's rational scientific information age." Paranormal research groups like the Cosmic Society of Paranormal Investigation provide a service for fans of these
shows who are not nearly as reluctant to consult ghost hunters as
they would have been a decade ago. "We get calls from doctors,
lawyers, businessmen, and families who can't talk to anyone in
their social groups for fear that they will be ostracized and stig-
matized," Brian says. "We've had calls from people who just never
believe in that stuff, yet they are having these experiences, and
finally they call the ghost hunters."

Donna believes that one of the primary charges leveled against
paranormal research groups—that they cannot agree on what the
paranormal is or how to go about investigating the paranormal—
should be viewed by investigations as a good thing: "Differences
of opinion are how we find things out," Donna says. "If everybody
would just work together and share results, [the field would really
advance]. How are we going to learn if we don't share our evidence? There are some groups who believe that knowledge is power
and they won't speak at this conference if so-and-so is going to be
there. Ego starts playing in and it gets distorted." Donna is thank-
ful that she has a good rapport with a number of ghost-hunting
groups: "I learn something every day, and I hope they learn from
me as well. Sometimes things I thought to be true twelve years
ago when I started are outdated—along with the equipment—

and new theories come along to replace the old ones. I'm open to working with other groups and sharing also. We aren't all as cold as the climate, like many people think."

In her quest to learn more about the paranormal, Donna has sought out several experts in the field to serve as mentors: "I have a very nice rapport with John Zaffis," Donna says. "He and I are like brother and sister. He started with the Warrens, and I worked with them as well thirteen years ago. That's when I met John." Because of her association with John Zaffis, Donna has been contacted by clergy seeking her assistance in cases that might be demonic. Her team also uses clergy in cases where spiritual assistance is required. "I have worked with Native American shamans too," Donna says. The evidence the Cosmic Society for Paranormal Investigation has collected over the years is impressive. "I have over two thousand photos," Donna said. "Many are photos others have given me to use. *Sightings* had sixty of my photos analyzed by Brooks Institute of Photography and could find no evidence of tampering." One of Donna's photographs of a man, which is labeled "Mr. P" on her web site, was voted by an organization as one of the top ten ghost photos of all time. On impulse, Donna stopped her car by a cemetery, jumped out, and took a picture of a grave. Later, a psychic who channeled the spirit of the man in the photograph gave Donna information that she would never have gotten otherwise. "The reason he showed up was because his father had killed someone in a drunken rage, and he needed help moving on," Donna said. "I guess in that brief second that I jumped out of the car and shot the picture in the cemetery, he foresaw that I would be working with a psychic who would help him move on." Coincidentally, the last name on the tombstone was "Peat." It turned out that the hotel where Donna was staying was on the Peat family property. Also, she learned that the man's family came from the same town in Pennsylvania that her mother was from.

The group collects other types of evidence as well. Some members of her group focus solely on EVPs. "I'm kind of bored with orbs," Donna says, "but I think they're the most basic way a spirit can present itself, so I don't discount them entirely." Photographs of orbs, which are discounted as unimportant by many groups, turned out to be very significant in 2005 in a case she had in Connecticut, where she and Brian took a large number of orb photographs. Afterward, Donna and Brian stopped at a restaurant for a bite to eat. For no apparent reason, Donna jumped out of her seat, ran out of the restaurant, and drove off in her car. Brian, who had taken his car also on the investigation, took off after her in hot pursuit. "She hit the curb and landed against a tree," Brian said. "I helped her out of the car and took her home. She didn't know what happened. In bed, I felt some kind of entity descend on Donna, so I said, 'You have no power over Donna. Get out of here!' The next day, a member called and played EVPs over the phone. 'Help her!' one screaming voice said. Another voice said, 'I'll get in the car!' I was so scared that I almost dropped the phone." The next day, while Donna was taking a shower, she noticed scratches forming on her arm. Grabbing her camera, she took a picture of the scratches before they disappeared. Brian theorizes that the entity attacked her because he was outside checking the damage to the car.

As harrowing as this experience was, it was not Donna's most memorable investigation. "There was an investigation in Philadelphia," Donna said. "We call it 'The Philly Poltergeist.' You can see the photos on the web site. This was a housing project type area. I was called in by a woman who lived on an old battlefield with her mother, herself, and her daughter, all with strong psychic abilities." Over the years, the women had had a number of sightings, including a soldier in the yard and something masquerading as a young child in the house. "Apparently, there was a murder across the street, a love-triangle sort of thing," Donna says. "Anyway, we were there setting up the equipment and things like that, and suddenly, I had the most 'poltergeist experience' I've ever witnessed in one setting. I would turn my back and turn around one second later, and one second later, all the cutlery was laid out on the table, perfectly placed. We also noticed that a curtain rod was taken off the window and placed in a doorway." Not long thereafter, the poltergeist turned its attention to the cats in the house. "They had three or four cats," Donna said. "We were watching the cats. Then, in the blink of an eye, one of the cats was walking around with leg holes and a tail hole made out of a plastic bread bag. We looked at one of the cats, then turned away for a second, and he was wearing this thing." At one point, the group lost track of the cats. The group searched all over the house but could not find the cats. Finally, one of the members happened to open the screen door and was surprised to find all three cats wedged between the closed front door and the screen door. Before the members left the house, the members began noticing that strange things had happened to several articles of clothing. Donna found a shirt that was tied up in knots so intricate that it took the group forty-five minutes to untie them. The strangest discovery of the evening was made in the freezer. "We opened the freezer, and we found underwear. Apparently, the underwear did not belong to anyone in the family. How crazy!" Donna said. The group obliged a woman who found out about the underwear in the freezer and requested that the photographs be placed on the group's web site.

Recently, the Cosmic Society of Paranormal Investigation has started branching out. The group now conducts ghost tours in Kelsey, Connecticut. Donna is embarking on a career as a writer. "The History Press has approached me," Donna said. "They let me focus on any place I chose in Connecticut. I'm writing a book about New London. I'm thinking of writing about Kelsey. They said if my New London book sells well, I can do the whole series."

PARANORMAL RESEARCH SOCIETY OF NEW ENGLAND
Stratford, Connecticut
John Zaffis, Director
www.prsne.com

John Zaffis grew up in a family who accepted the paranormal as a matter of course. The nephew of pioneering paranormal researchers Ed and Lorraine Warren, John did not begin to think seriously about ghosts until he saw his first ghost: "I was about fifteen or sixteen years old when I had a sighting at the foot of my bed," John says. "It was transparent, and was shaking its head back and forth. I got startled and ran downstairs and told my Mom about it, and she asked me if it did anything or said anything, and I said, 'No, it just stood there and shook its head back and forth.' And she looked at me with this complex look on her face and said, 'Well that was your grandfather.' I said, 'How do you know that was your father?' And she said, 'Dad used to shake his head back and forth if something was wrong or if he was upset.' After she told me about her father, I became intrigued." John began asking himself questions, such as "Why are these things happening?" and "Why are certain people experiencing these things?" He began reading every book he could about ghosts and demons. He also began visiting haunted locations and going on investigations. Years later, John recalled that his grandmother passed away a couple of days after he saw the ghost of his grandfather. He now wonders if his grandfather appeared to help his grandmother, who lived with John and his parents, cross over. "That's one of those magical things we are still trying to figure out," John says.

After studying under the Warrens, John's interest in the paranormal became more specialized. He began focusing more on demonology and participated in exorcisms. For the past thirty years, John has worked with Roman Catholic priests, monks, Buddhists, rabbis, ministers, and some of the best-known exorcists in the world, including Malachi Martin, Robert McKenna, and the Reverend Jun. He has been featured in several books written by Ed and Lorraine Warren and has written two books about ghosts, demons, and possession, titled *Shadows of the Dark* and *The Trouble Within*. John has also been featured in several television programs, including the NBC series *Unsolved Mysteries* and the Discovery Channel documentaries *Little Lost Souls* and *Haunting in Connecticut*. He currently co-hosts the *Paranormal Nights* radio show with Brendan Keenan and makes guest appearances on the *Beyond Reality* radio show, hosted by TAPS's Jason Hawes and Grant Wilson.

Before he began devoting most of his time to paranormal research, John's profession was quality control/engineering. "Years ago, you didn't discuss [the paranormal]," John said. "You didn't bring it up." For a long time, very few of John's coworkers knew that he went out on investigations at night or on the weekend.

However, he could not longer keep his after-work activities a secret after the exposure he began receiving from books and television: "Before long, people started associating the face with the name. In the beginning, people did not like discussing it, but as time went on, on Monday mornings in the coffee klatsch, everyone wanted to know what I did over the weekend. So interest in what I was doing developed at work." John believes that his engineering background has given him the skills required to properly document an investigation.

The Paranormal Research Society of New England looks at paranormal occurrences from both the scientific viewpoint and the spiritual viewpoint. John says, "Back when we started investigating, we relied heavily on mediums and psychics to be able to give us information, and hopefully, we had enough information enough to fit the pieces of the puzzle together to figure out the haunting. Today, my group has fifteen members, and six of them are sensitives. I like to integrate psychics and mediums and with people who walk around with the tape recorders, checking to see if there are hot or cold spots, and who use infrared cameras that document and verify what the sensitives are picking up on. I like to use all the tools that are available." Even though John truly believes that the metaphysical approach is a viable method of investigating the paranormal, he refuses to use dowsing rods or Ouija boards. "I am a firm believer in doing things naturally. By doing things naturally, you'll get some type of result eventually," John says.

John's hybrid approach to investigating the paranormal is reflected in his attitude toward EVPs, which he admits neither he nor anyone else totally understands: "We know that certain individuals have the ability to get these recordings, and others don't get them. I've never gotten one. It's very frustrating. I've brought new people in with me, and they are getting EVPs like crazy, and I never get them." EVPs by themselves are adequate proof that a site is haunted. "I look at everything as a whole," John says. "I take a lot of things into consideration. If we're getting EVPs, I want to see if they are anything we can use to solve the riddle of the haunting." When John's group does record an EVP, he always is always very guarded when he plays it back for the clients; instead of telling them what they should be hearing, he waits for them to say what *they* think they are hearing.

John believes that orbs are much less reliable than EVPs as evidence because 95 percent of them are dust or moisture. "But when you are in a room, and you are getting temperature changes, and photographs produce orbs that are solid, then I look at that a little differently," John says. Genuine orbs, he feels, are spirit energy, not ghosts.

John and his group go into an investigation with an open mind. "I always look for logic," John says. "When someone tells me, 'I just moved this house a month ago, and we've been hearing bangings and other noises, ninety-nine percent of the time, you are going to find a logical explanation. If it's something logical [that is causing the disturbances], boy, does that make my life easy! If there are squirrels or mice in the walls, and we can prove that, they call the exterminator, and I go home and we're all taken care of. That's an easy fix, but it also helps people understand what is happening to them." John says that even before the investigation when he is making initial contact with the clients on the telephone, he tells them to see if there might be a "down-to-earth" reason for the activity. Most people are relieved when he explains to them a logical explanation for the haunting. More and people today, though, seem to be in love with the idea of sharing their house with a ghost. "Today we have to be very careful because we're becoming like Ireland and Scotland and England, where everyone wants a ghost in their house," John says. "So our view systems have changed a lot. People don't fear the paranormal like they used to. They look at it differently, so we have to do things differently when we do investigations."

John credits the popularity of the *Ghost Hunters* television show with making people more receptive to the possibility that the paranormal really exists. "The popularity of the *Ghost Hunters* TV show has made people more willing to allow paranormal investigators into their homes," says John, who is a member of the TAPS family. "I've been on the show a couple of times. I'm very good friends with Jason. We are buddies. We go way back long before he became involved in paranormal investigating." John feels an affinity with Jason and Grant because they, too, go into an investigation looking for a logical explanation: "They try to debunk things from a realistic perspective, and I can understand that. I look at that open-mindedly, and I feel that the TV series has opened up the doors for people to understand things, and that has been a very, very important step forward in the paranormal field." Although John admits that there is a difference between what happens on televised investigations and what happens on actual investigations, the "drama" that erupts occasionally is real: "And believe me, I know how it gets behind the scenes with the groups—they tear each other apart. It gets nasty. You got a tremendous amount of character influences in the personalities and our field is extremely competitive."

However, if John and his group do not collect evidence at a site, they do not tell their clients that their house is not haunted. "I revisit it, especially if I am doing a private residence," John says. "You can go back three or four times before you finally hear those scratches or knocking sounds that the client has been hearing. If you don't get some sort of evidence, that doesn't mean that these people aren't going through some sort of haunting. I have been known to go back several times on an investigation because I am looking for a reason why the haunting is happening."

John admits that his group has run into conflict with the religious community in the past, primarily because of John's specialization in demonology. He believes that today, though, religious people are much more receptive to the possibility that ghosts and demons exist. For this reason, he has had no trouble recruiting clergy to assist him with his investigations. "I use clergy all the time," John says. "I've worked with Roman Catholic priests, Buddhists, ministers, rabbis, shamans—there aren't very many clergy I haven't integrated over the years. I will do clearings—what I call cleansings or bindings—but as far as exorcisms over an individual are concerned, absolutely not. That's a job for the clergy."

John's mission is to help people when he and his group go out on a case: "When you go into a stressful situation, your investigation can give them peace of mind," John says. Just recently, though, John found out that not all of his members feel the same way he does: "The group was sitting around, and I asked them what was their main objective, why did they join a paranormal group, and everybody basically comes up with same answer—they want that hard core proof that there is an existence after we leave this physical body. That is the main goal of most people who get involved with this group." Despite the fact that John and the members of his group are not always "on the same page," they have still managed to help hundreds of people over the years.

As John's group began doing more investigations in private residences, he realized that he could help people better if he was familiar with a variety of religions: "I studied Buddhism, shamans, rabbis, ministers—all I tried to integrate and understand to be able help get the people out over time." Circumstances and the individual client dictate whether or not John asks the clients their religious affiliations. He laments the fact that many of his clients who are experiencing problems with demons in their house have no religious beliefs at all. "A lot of people don't have belief systems," John says. "They don't believe in God, let alone believe on a negative level. So you have to look at everything from a whole and be very open-minded to be able to understand the different perspectives that people go through or are involved with. Then if I am working with a religious person, I by all means follow the doctrine of what they practice."

The Paranormal Research Society of New England also conducts investigation at historical sites. "I love doing historical places," John says. "Gettysburg is one of my favorite places. I also love going to Old Fort Mifflin down in Philadelphia. The oldest established areas are so intriguing to go in and investigate." John enjoys investigating historical places because, as a rule, a lot of activity takes place at these sites. However, John has no patience with those groups who go into a historically haunted site for three or four hours without finding any evidence and then conclude that the place is not haunted: "I very seldom agree with that," John says. "If you have an old house that is two or three hundred years old, and a lot of people have gotten evidence from those locations over the years, then it is ridiculous for a group who has been there once to say that it is not haunted. Most of the time, you will have some sort of paranormal activity that will transpire in these places."

John's most interesting investigations are those dealing with possession, especially those cases in which there is some type of outward manifestation, like demonic voices. "I have been witness to that several times," John says. He is also intrigued by poltergeist cases involving objects moving by themselves, spontaneous fires, or even rain inside a house. When investigating these cases, John tries to determine if the activity is being caused by poltergeists or by psychokinesis (PK): "When any of us say that these adolescents responsible for poltergeist activity engage in PK unconsciously, these kids are very much aware of it. They are very much aware of what they are doing. They keep it a secret. A lot of times during an investigation, things will happen, and I'll turn and look at them and say, 'I know you did that.' And they get startled and say, 'How does he know that?' And I'll just chuckle." When John is investigating a house where a poltergeist is said to be active, he looks for an ozone smell, which he says indicates PK: "A lot of poltergeist cases I just rule out as PK—nothing paranormal about it as well." He cites the Bell Witch as the most famous poltergeist case in the United States. He was very disappointed, however, by the movie that was based on the case, *An American Haunting*: "A lot of us in the field study these cases for years, and when Hollywood makes a movie out of them, we look at each other and say, 'Huh?'"

For John Zaffis, the ability to look at a case from different perspectives is a definite asset for paranormal investigators: "The biggest thing with me is I always try to stay open-minded, and I always try to understand things from every point of view because here again, if we don't come outside of our box, we're really not learning anything." Is it important for John to prove the existence of the paranormal scientifically? "Oh, absolutely!" John responds.

CONNECTICUT PARANORMAL
RESEARCH TEAM
Groton, Connecticut
Coby Baldouf, Director
www.ctparanormal.com

C oby Baldouf is one of many paranormal investigators whose curiosity was piqued by growing up in a haunted house. "We always knew something was there," Coby said. "We heard footsteps walking up and down the hallway. Sometimes, I heard somebody banging on my door at two or three in the morning. My parents would come up with these lame explanations, like 'It's the house settling.' One time, when it happened in the summer, my mother said, 'Don't worry. It's just the air conditioner changing gears.' Even when I was six or seven, her explanations didn't make any sense to me." Sometimes, relatives who visited Coby's home also had strange experiences. "I remember my cousins asking me one time who the guy was standing at the top of the stairs." His cousins' sighting verified what Coby had always suspected: that the spirit inhabiting their house was a male.

Growing up in a haunted house might have been fun for Coby and his sister, but some of his girlfriends did not share his affection for the place. "I used to bring my girlfriends to the house, and one of them saw a shadow pass through the bottom of the basement door," Coby said. "She freaked out! She came running up to me and said, 'I don't know if I can come over here anymore.' She was really scared. I tried to calm her down; I told her that it was only a shadow, but she didn't buy it." Coby could not really empathize with the poor girl because he and his sister had grown accustomed to living with a ghost.

Coby founded the Connecticut Paranormal Research Team in 2005. "We were part of another group before that, but that group broke up," Coby said. His eight-member group includes a licensed psychotherapist, a human resources representative, and a plumber, who comes in very handy when clients report hearing strange noises. The group's overriding mission is to find evidence of the paranormal. "We look for what's credible," Coby says. "We rule out every possible explanation, and we try to find out what else [the phenomena] could be besides a ghost or spirit." On one investigation, the group recorded thirteen hours of video. After viewing the tape and ruling out every anomaly that could be dust, the group ended up with less than a minute of footage that was credible. "When people ask me what ghost hunting is like, I tell them that it is a lot like fishing," Coby says. "You might be sitting in a rain storm and not catch anything. [Ghost hunting] is a very painstaking process. It's not exactly action-packed all the time. I admit that it's pretty exciting when you do find something credible, but you might have to stare eight to ten hours at the video of a table or chair in order to see it." Needless to say, prospective members are often disillusioned when Coby informs them that investigating is boring much, if not most, of the time.

Coby posts evidence on the group's web site only if it is backed up with other evidence. Orbs that are captured on video, for example, are much more meaningful if the EMF (electromotive force) meter is registering spikes at the same time. Coby has viewed so many hours of video footage, however, that he has developed the ability to discern genuine orbs and flecks of dust or lint. To test his theory that most orbs are dust, Coby conducted an experiment in his apartment: "I hooked up all the cameras like I was doing an investigation. I turned on the air conditioner and took footage of dust floating around with my infrared camera." Genuine orbs, Coby says, are characterized by rapid starts and stops. They also have the ability to change directions: "Orbs could be ghosts or some phenomenon that science has not classified yet. There are a lot of unknowns in this field."

Coby believes that growing up in a haunted house has made him impervious to most of the potentially frightening situations he has found himself in. EVPs, on the other hand, creep him out. "There's just no explanation for EVPs," Coby says. "It's really hard even for skeptics to dismiss EVPs. I've heard some skeptics come up with explanations that don't even make any sense, like radio interference. EVPs are critical once you have ruled out any other noises." One of the most unsettling EVPs Coby has ever heard was recorded in his parents' house. "It was around Easter. I had my mom flip on the recorder before she went to bed," Coby says. "You can hear a voice say, 'The house is full. We can't get out!' It's a really clear EVP."

Although the Connecticut Paranormal Research Team has investigated a few private residences, Coby prefers going to places that are historically haunted because the chances of capturing evidence are better. One of the team's most memorable investigations was conducted in one of these historical sites. Coby was walking around an old cemetery when he and some of the other members caught sight of a bright "ribbon of light" soaring through the air. "It was as bright as a neon light," Coby said. "It was six or seven feet off the ground and was only a foot or two long. It lasted only about two seconds." Unfortunately, Coby was unable to set up his video camera in time to film the phenomenon. He thinks that his group might have encountered the spirit of a British soldier, who is said to pace up and down the dirt road that passes by the cemetery.

The spirit that haunts the old graveyard showed up again later that same night. The team had parked their car on the road with the door propped open. "I walked over to the car to get my thirty-five-millimeter camera out, "Coby said. "I took a few pictures with it and was going to put it back in the truck and switch to video. As I was taking a few more pictures, the truck door slammed shut in front of us. There were at least five or six members of the group who witnessed it." Coby tried to replicate the phenomenon that night and the following door. "We left the door exactly the same way it was. I gently pushed it with my fingers, but I couldn't get it to close. The only way I could get the door to shut the same way it did the night before was by shoving the door closed with so much pressure that the entire truck rocked. The truck hardly moved at all the night before when the door shut."

On an investigation in a private residence, Coby and his group experienced activity that could have been generated by a poltergeist: "The group was in the kitchen when a glass that was upside down in a dish drainer jumped out of the sink and smashed onto the floor. It was a short, squat juice glass that somehow managed to get out of the dish drainer and on to the floor with enough force that [the glass] broke into a million pieces. I was in the next room when it happened. It was pretty amazing."

Gettysburg National Military Park also produced some startling evidence. The first year the team visited the battlefield, Coby had a very weird experience after the investigation. "I took six and a half hours to drive down there, and I was dead tired," Coby said. "We did some investigating that night, and we were all tired. We went to bed at a country inn, but at two o'clock, I woke up. It was a very strange feeling, like a panic attack. My chest felt really tight. Somehow, I managed to get my camera and take some pictures." The next day, the group once again conducted a nighttime investigation. Coby went to sleep at 1:00 A.M. at the same inn; an hour later, he woke up again. This time, his EMF detector was within close reach. "It's a special type," Coby said. "It's quiet. When it registers an anomaly, it flashes instead of beeping. Well, this thing was going off like a Christmas tree. The hair was standing up on the back of my neck. I grabbed my video camera and started filming, but I didn't catch anything." The next day, the landlady asked Coby how he spent the night; he told her that he woke up at exactly 2:00 A.M. for two nights in a row. The landlady replied, "Oh, that happens to everybody who tries to sleep in that particular room." Coby told her that he was awakened not by a physical sensation, like pinching, but by a very stressful feeling.

Coby had an even more bizarre experience on the group's next visit to Gettysburg the following year. Coby was sitting on the battlefield with another member, Scott, when he saw a man headed down a hill in his direction. The man walked up to Coby and said, "Something is going on up there. I couldn't take it anymore, so I decided to come down." Coby turned to Scott and said, "I'm going up there." The entire time Coby was walking up the hill, he thought Scott was behind him, carrying the camcorder. When Coby reached the top of the hill, he began taking a few photographs and some meter readings when he noticed a figure standing next to him. "He was about six feet tall," Coby said. "Where the head should have been was a dull, red light, about the size of a softball. I immediately thought it was Scott with his camcorder and the red light was his night vision. So I stood there for a while, and I was talking to this figure: 'Scott, let's check over here. I've been getting some really weird readings, and I got some orbs with the camera.' So I started walking back down the hill to the car, and the whole time, I felt like something was right behind me. I didn't see Scott anymore, so I went back down the hill, and my hair was standing on the back of my neck. I looked at the car, and there was Scott. I said, 'Scott, wasn't that crazy up there? I got a great picture of an orb.' He looked at me like I was crazy and said, 'What are you talking about? I didn't go up there. I've been down here with the car the entire time. You were the only one who was up there. Everyone else was down here.'" At that moment, Coby realized that he had been in the presence of a ghost.

On a third trip to Gettysburg, Coby was in the Spangler's Springs area of the park with one other person. "They were calling us to go back down to the car," Coby said. "I could see someone sitting on a rock farther down the trail in a grassy area. I thought it was somebody from the group. It looked like he was wearing a white, hooded sweatshirt. I couldn't make out any other details because he was two hundred feet away. The trail curved around for a second, and a tree was blocking my vision. When I passed the tree, the spirit was gone from the rock." After recovering from his initial shock, Coby surmised that either the man on the rock was an extremely fast runner, or he was actually a ghost.

Coby has encountered a number of unfriendly spirits on his investigations, but he does not believe that all of them were demons. Many people who claim to have been attacked by demons were investigating old prisons or insane asylums. "There have even been cases where people have been pushed down the stairs or been scratched or have had their hair pulled in a prison. One thing I tell my members is that spirits act exactly the same way they did when they were alive. If you are in a prison full of the spirits of murderers or rapists, chances are good that you are not going to run into anything good while you are there." Coby believes that there is such a thin line between demons and bad people that he doesn't even try to distinguish between the two. "I just say, 'He's evil,' and let it go at that," Coby says.

Despite the fact that Coby has had more than his shares of paranormal experiences, he does not consider himself to be a psychic: "I think you become sensitive after a while if you keep going to places that are haunted. After a while, you can tell a haunted location from a nonhaunted location. A haunted location feels heavy. You can also feel the static energy in the air in a really haunted location. I know something is going on if the hair is standing on the back of my neck." Like most ghost hunters, Coby puts more faith in his EMF detectors and his temperature meters than in his psychic abilities.

PARANORMAL INVESTIGATION GROUP OF NEW ENGLAND
Plainfield, Connecticut
Tabitha Denihan, Director
www.pig-ne.com

Tabitha Denihan did not become really interested in ghosts until she was in high school: "A friend of mine said she lived in a haunted house, and I experienced a few things there, like weird feelings and shadow people. Then in 1999, I met my ex-boyfriend. We started dating, and he had his own informal group. He started dragging me along, and after six months of doing this, I got hooked." After investigating the paranormal for ten years in different groups, Tabitha finally decided to found her own group in March 2007. The Paranormal Investigation Group of New England has between twenty-five and thirty members. The members include a manager for Olympia Sports, a small business owner, a employee of Agway, an electrician, two college students, a writer for the Associated Press, and a retired couple. Tabitha, who is a stay-at-home mom, has to juggle the demands of motherhood with her caseload. "[When I go out on an investigation at night], I have to make sure my fiancé is home to be with the baby, but if we go out to a few different sites during the day to see if we want to conduct an investigation there, I bring him along. When I do investigations at night, sometimes I don't get back home until three A.M., and the baby is up at six A.M., so that makes my sleep schedule really short." As a rule, the group conducts one investigation each month.

The mission of the the Paranormal Investigation Group of New England is to help people. "In high school, when my friend was growing up, I saw what a hard time she had living in a haunted house," Tabitha says. "I always thought to myself, 'Wouldn't it be nice if there was someone out there who could help them deal with this issue, whatever it ends up being?' If it is not a haunting, you can put their minds at rest. If it is a haunting, you can at least let them know what is going on." Proving the existence of the paranormal is a secondary goal because Tabitha is already convinced that it exists. However, she does look forward to the day when the field of parapsychology will gain more respectability. "That is one of the goals we have set for ourselves," Tabitha says, "to help the field of paranormal research become more accepted instead of being viewed as a laughingstock science."

The Paranormal Investigation Group of New England has four members who are sensitives, but Tabitha does not advertise the fact: "I am sensitive, and so is my aunt, Deborah, and my sister, Nicole. I am a little clairvoyant, but mostly clairaudient when I sense spirits. Nicole has been known to experience prophetic dreaming. Susan, one of our other members, is quite sensitive herself and does Tarot readings. We don't use the sensitives on our team as our primary source for gathering evidence, though." The kind of evidence that Tabitha's group is after is what she calls the "cold, hard stuff," in other words, scientific proof. Her group refuses to use dowsing rods, for example, because she prefers methods that have been validated scientifically. This is not to say, though, that she dismisses metaphysical evidence entirely. "We have no problem posting our personal experiences on our web site," Tabitha says, "but we don't use them as the sole judge."

Because the Paranormal Investigation Group of New England is fairly new, "getting the word out there" is critical. "Senior members can have their own business cards, and then we have the regular ones for the other members," Tabitha says. "We also do classes in ghost hunting at two stores, the Weight Shop and Delilah's." The group also teaches a Ghost Hunting 101 class at the local community college. "In the first class, we go over the history of ghost hunting. In the second class, we go into the more advanced stuff, like the kind of equipment we use, how to get EVPs, and how to get a true photograph. Then at the end, we take the class to a haunted location, like a cemetery," Tabitha says. Tabitha has also recruited two members of her group from these classes, including Rick Anthony, whose military background has afforded him a variety of skills that come in handy on investigations.

Tabitha's group is currently investigating historic sites, for the most part, until the Paranormal Investigation Group of New England becomes better known. At the time of the interview, the most recent historic site the group had investigated was a Masonic Lodge. "The building has been standing for a hundred and fifty years. We got a ton of activity at that place," Tabitha said. "We might have gotten a semiformed apparition on digital camera too. One of our members had a Sony Nightshot camcorder, and she said that when she was upstairs, she recorded a stream of orbs flying around faster than dust can move." The group captured several startling EVPs as well, including a voice that said, "Read all about it." Deborah, the group's case manager, could not understand why a spirit would say something like this. She was shocked when the tech department manager revealed that *The Journal Transcript* was formerly published at this particular site. "We didn't know that. That was really amazing," Tabitha said. Midway through the investigation, the group sensed that the spirits in one particular room did not want to be photographed. Tabitha said, "I was doing some EVP work, so I asked the spirits if they wanted to be photographed. I asked them to make some sort of discernible noise for us. Suddenly, we all heard a tapping noise. Like something tapping their nails on a chair. There were chairs in there, but no one was near them, and the room was pretty well sealed off." Incredibly, none of the members seemed to be frightened by the spirits' way of acknowledging their presence in the room.

During another investigation at a different site, five members were in a room relaxing because they were unable to collect any evidence there. At the time, the door was shut. "I was sitting there, looking at the door, because I was getting the impression that it was starting to open." All at once, Tabitha could contain herself no longer: "I said, 'Is that open or shut because I swear to God, I saw someone peeking in the door.' One member said, 'No, that's Chuck.' Right after that, we recorded an EVP saying, 'I'm all around the room.' I was so excited when I heard it. I wasn't expecting to get a reply." Later on, Tabitha found out that someone in another group had seen someone peeking in at the door.

Ghost hunters, for the most part, are ordinary people. They take time from their jobs and their families to investigate the paranormal. Tabitha Denihan is a good example of a person for whom investigating is more than just a hobby. It's a genuine passion.

AWARE FOUNDATION:
PARANORMAL RESEARCH
Waterbury, Connecticut
Reverend Larry Elward, Director
www.angelfire.com/scifi/deliverances

Larry Elward is the director of a very small paranormal research. The group consists of Larry, his wife, and John Zaffis, the director of the Paranormal Research Society of New England. Both Larry and his wife, Debbie, are ordained independent priests. "I don't have a church per se," Larry says. "We did get some flak from the Catholic church in the beginning because I was still a Catholic, but I was not a priest at the time. I was ordained by a bishop with both Catholic and Eastern Orthodox lineage, so I am pretty much independent now. They can't really criticize me anymore."

The members of AWARE conduct paranormal investigations and also perform exorcisms. "When we are investigating a house, it is usually just a homebound or earthbound spirit that just needs to be guided to the light," Larry said. "This is pretty much what Debbie does. You don't really need an exorcist to do this." When the group is called to a house in which someone is suffering from demonic possession, Larry takes over. "My wife and I feel threatened quite often," Larry says. "We perform one exorcism per month, on the average." Larry was featured in an episode on the Discovery Channel series *A Haunting* in 2006. The episode, which was titled "The Possessed," was about a possessed woman who levitated. "She was sitting in a chair, and she levitated," Larry said. "We were working with John Zaffis on that one. They interviewed him too. I was on only for about four seconds. I was portrayed by an actor for the greater part of the show, and that 'ain't bad.'" Larry was not really frightened during the exorcism because he was saying prayers most of the time and was not really concentrating on what was going on around him. It was only after the fact that it was brought to his attention that the woman was levitating. "The chair was not levitating," Larry said. "She was climbing over the chair, and everyone was grabbing her and pulling her down. It was only after we analyzed the tape that we found that she was actually rising. My wife was trying to keep the poor girl in the chair, and she was psychically involved as well. If I were psychic, I would not be able to do what I'm doing. I would be 'watching the show,' or the 'floor show,' as we like to say. My wife watches the floor show, and I do the prayers. Our marriage is made in heaven. We fight like cats and dogs, but we are doing the Lord's work."

Debbie can distinguish between the presence of ghosts or demons. She can tell what's there and how many spirits are there. "Most apparitions materialize like mist forms," Larry says. "Demonic entities appear as dark, shadowy figures. The portrayal of the exorcism in *The Exorcist* is Hollywood, but it's pretty close to reality. We've had vomiting, but it's more like the dry heaves, not green pea soup. We have had the profanity. The possessed person will change, but it won't be as horrific as it was portrayed in the movie. The demon does not want to show itself, but it does want to show that it is there." Most of Larry's exorcisms are effective, but sometimes he has to return a second or third time. Exorcising demons is personally satisfying for Larry because most of the time his clients are very grateful. "They tell us that their lives are transformed," Larry said.

Larry and his group do not receive very much publicity when they are doing an exorcism because most people want to keep it to themselves. "We appreciate their need for privacy," Larry said. "We don't exploit anybody. We do exorcisms as part of our ministry. But we are paranormal investigators also. How that works hand-in-hand, I can't really say, but it does." Aside from driving out demons, Larry would also like to prove the existence of the paranormal. "We try to use the scientific method to prove the theological," Larry says. "We find no conflict between religious doctrine and what I do. Historically, Christianity has not been afraid of archaeologists trying to disprove the Bible, so why should we try to disprove theology through modern, scientific methods? My investigations solidify my faith."

One of the few historic sites that AWARE has investigated is the site of the hanging of a witch in Bridgeport, Connecticut. "Her name was Goody Knapp," Larry says, "She was apparently a simple-minded woman who talked to her herself. She was hanged in 1653 at the corner of Fairfield Avenue and Ellsworth Street, which is what the area is called now. We are pretty sure that they buried her where they hanged her." Several years ago, Larry and Debbie were driving past the site, and Larry said, "A witch was hanged there years ago. Her name was Goody Knapp." At that very moment, Larry thought he saw a woman hanging from a gallows. He found out later that a few other people have also seen the ghost of the hanging woman. Apparently, Goody Knapp is so grateful that Larry and Debbie are trying to get her exonerated that she moved in with them. "My wife saw her in our house when we lived in Bridgeport," Larry said. "We were talking about having her exonerated, and she said, 'Thank you.' Debbie also saw her digging in our clothes basket. You can't make this up!"

AWARE does not charge for its investigations, but sometimes Larry wishes that it did: "We just about went broke recently driving down to Huntsville, Alabama, at our own expense. We went to Montreal at our own expense. We had a good time. We have been through some Southern battlefields and graveyards. People are so nice down there. You go into a store, and they say, 'How are you? How are you doing?' and they wait for you to say, 'How are you?' and they mean it."

Despite the expense, Larry Elward will continue working with AWARE, not only because he wants to help people, but also because he enjoys it: "What I like is that I keep one foot in this world and one foot in the other world, and I am not afraid to use cameras and tape recorders and things like that." He feels a close kinship to the New England witches because they, like him, were in close touch with the world of the paranormal. The difference is that they were burned at the stake.

MAINE

BANGOR GHOST HUNTERS ASSOCIATION
Greenbush, Maine
Harold Murray, Director
www.bangormaineghosthuntersassociation.com

Harold Murray had a paranormal experience when he was young, but that is not what turned him into a paranormal investigator. "Watching the Travel Channel, the Discovery Channel, the Learning Channel—this is what did it," Harold says. "Every year, they have these specials on. I'm a retired magician, and I wanted to see what it could do. I wanted to see if this stuff could be explained. So I started taking pictures and started using tri-field readers and we started picking up stuff. The next thing we know, Maine Paranormal contacted us. They liked what we had, and they offered us their northern branch in 2000. As we were learning, we were finding out that much of this stuff could be explained, but it was the unexplained stuff that really got us into it."

Harold founded his team in 2000. Most of his investigators are family members. "My son, John Murray, is the co-director. He started out with Northern Maine as a cameraman. He did video interviews with people," Harold said. Recently, Harold has looked outside of the family for talented people. "We are always looking for somebody who can do it better," Harold said. "We just brought in a new team member who is a professional photographer." One of his members, Spike, is a gold prospector. He uses his dowsing rods to measure the electric and magnetic fields of the earth. Harold believes Spike is more accurate than the team's tri-field meters: "He's been with us for a year now. He uses rods made of copper, steel, iron, bronze, and a couple of other metals. He makes them himself. It's pretty impressive what he does." Harold, who is an ordained minister, carries holy water and the Bible with him on investigation in case the team runs into a demonic entity. Harold has no psychics in his group. "I have had some psychics apply to be on our team," Harold says. "I tell them I'll take psychics. I give them a psychic test I have at home. 'If you can tell me what is in each of these envelopes, I'll take you along as a psychic. Otherwise, you're just a field investigator.' For some reason, they don't come back. Actually, this test does not exist. I just made it up." From Harold's viewpoint, Sylvia Browne is probably the only genuine psychic.

Harold maintains that the team members are the most important members of the team: "The *Ghost Hunters* television show makes it look like the director is the most important part of the team, but that's not true. You have your field investigators, you have your lead investigators, you have your researchers, you have your cameraman, you have your technical support, you have your computer guy. These people are not mentioned in all the stories about TAPS. The team is important to me. I can't do it alone. It's not a two-man operation." The group holds its monthly meetings at the Bangor Museum. All of its meetings are open to the general public.

Sometimes, overly enthusiastic members can jeopardize the validity of an investigation. Several years ago, Harold's oldest son accompanied Harold and a reporter on an investigation."My son thought he was doing good for us," Harold said. "He faked an EVP. This did not go over too well with me, and I exposed him in front of the reporter. And he is not allowed to be a member of the team because he pulled this stunt. This is how serious I am about ghost hunting." Harold's son John also fabricated evidence. "He sent two videotapes to the head office in northern Maine, but he was practicing magic. He took an orange seed with a prop that we use, videotaped it, sent it down to them and told them it was a ghost. They believed it and posted it on the Internet. My son finally went down with me and showed them how the trick was done. They felt like asses, but they couldn't retract it because they didn't want to look like fools," Harold says. Because Harold knows how easy it is to fake evidence, he does not take EVPs or videotape or pictures off the Internet. "Anything that comes to me has to be in negative form or the actual videotape because we don't want any hoaxes," Harold says.

Bangor Ghost Hunters Association uses a variety of scientific equipment in their investigations, including tri-field meters, digital and analog cassette recorders, analog VHS and digital VHS, infrared thermometers, digital Hi8, booster mikes, and laptop computers. The group also uses metal detectors, cell phones, and walkie-talkies. Most of this stuff is donated to the team, but Harold has picked up some old videocassette recorders (VCRs) and cameras at yard sales.

Most of the group's clients find out about Bangor Ghost Hunters Association through word of mouth. "If people in town say a house is haunted and new people move in and know nothing about the house, the first thing they're going to hear is a neighbor will tell them, 'Oh, you live in a haunted house. I heard someone died there.' Then the power of suggestion takes over, and every noise in the new house, the people think the house is haunted," Harold said. A large number of the group's clients seem to feel that an investigation by a group of paranormal researchers is a quick fix to a serious problem. Harold blames TAPS for giving the general public this impression: "We see TAPS and the other ghost hunters on TV, and they only spend one night there. We tell our clients that we could be here for a day or we could be here every weekend for six months. It took us six months to catch something in a house in Old Town. Up here in Maine, we have strong weather. A good, strong wind will make a house creak. A lot of the stuff they have here like the old stone wall basements have minerals that will affect the electromagnetic fields. Electromagnetic fields do affect brain waves and make people hear and see things that they can't explain."

Very few of the places the group investigates are actually haunted, however. "We give out certificates if we have enough evidence that the house has paranormal activity going on, and we have only given out two since 2000," Harold says. "The certificates don't mean that the house is haunted, though. They just mean that something is going on that we can't explain."

All of the group's investigations begin with an interview. "We interview our clients on the phone or in person," Harold says. "While the interview is being conducted, we send another member around the neighborhood to gather information on the house and the land to see if anybody really died there. Then after we do our interview, we meet up with the member who tried to get information about the house. We meet up at my house and get everybody's opinions to see what they thought about the house. We then look into the legal limits of the family to see if they are credible people. We don't get involved with people if they have had trouble with the law."

Before the group begins an investigation, Harold goes in with a cameraman, and they do a sweep. "The cameraman follows me around, and being a retired magician, I look for 'smoke and mirrors'—strings and everything else," Harold says. "I have come across speakers in walls. These are people who do haunted houses at Halloween. And a lot of them do it to see if the ghost hunters are on the up-and-up. We had this one case where there were strings and speakers in the walls, and I told the owner, 'You have no haunting here. You know what you're doing. You're trying to run a ruse.' The gentleman said, 'Yes, I am, but I wanted to see if you guys were on the up-and-up.' He was testing our people. He was a follower of Henry Houdini. Houdini tried to debunk the fake séances, and I do the same thing, but I don't look for fake psychics. I look for fake haunted houses." If everything turns out clean, Harold sends in his team to do the initial investigation. They go through the house one more time, looking for things that Harold might have overlooked. Then the group sits down and starts videotaping and recording EVPs. "We use boom mikes attached to tape recorders that will pick up the lightest sound two houses away," Harold says.

The Bangor Ghost Hunters Association has done investigations at a variety of sites, including a school, supermarkets, a bank, bars, a cemetery, and several homes. "We even went to a haunted gold mine in Maine. Maine does have gold mines. Most people don't realize that," Harold said. Some of the members are eager to become part of the TAPS family so that they can get more cases, but Harold is reluctant. "I think we are getting enough," Harold said. "I'm booked right now until June with cases. Once is an old funeral home that was turned into a restaurant called 'The Fountain House.' We were doing a radio show last year on Halloween, and they asked us to come down there and investigate."

Harold has learned the hard way that printed legends are not always good indicators of where to look for haunted places. "Every book that is published about haunted locations, we go out and check them," Harold says. "I have a book that says a cemetery in Indian Island is haunted. I went out there and talked to the elders, and I never had a Native American look me in the face before and tell me I was 'f——ing crazy.' I showed him the article in the book, and he was surprised it was published because he didn't know anything about it. He checked with the elders, and none of them had heard the story that was published in the book. We talked to ten elders, and they asked us if we were crazy or if we had been drinking whiskey. We like trying to get trying to get evidence to corroborate these published stories. I don't know why a lot of this stuff gets published."

Harold's innate skepticism enabled him to expose another client who was trying to "pull a con": "I was sitting in a bar talking about another case I was working on in Massachusetts. A gentleman overheard our conversation. He came up to me and apologized for eavesdropping, but he said he was experiencing unexplained phenomena—noises and lights. It turns out that that's all it was—noises and lights. There were no ghosts or anything. I went through the house, and I found speakers and a prop that would be used in a light show on stage. A magic shop was the only place in Boston where you could buy this stuff. I contacted them, and they remembered me and I asked for a list of people who bought a certain type of equipment and props. He gave me the list, and the gentleman's son was on that list. I contacted the son. He tried to deny what was going on, but I told him I had gone down to the magic shop and found out that he had bought all of this equipment. He said, 'If I come clean, what's going to happen to me?' I said, 'It's not against the law, but I think you should come clean because you gave your father a heart attack and put him in the hospital.' He said he did it out of revenge for his father's years of tormenting him and his brother by saying, 'The ghosts are coming to get you!' or 'The bogeyman is coming to get you.' I guess this had gone on since he was fifteen years old. He was about twenty when he did it. He's now twenty-two years old. The kid finally got even."

After the man was released from the hospital, he and his son did not speak for six months. By now, enough time has passed that the man thinks the incident was funny. His son, however, feels guilty for giving his father a heart attack.

A store in Holland, Maine, was the site of another fabricated haunting. The group was investigating reports that the store was being haunted by the ghost of the store owner, who was an avid hunter. "He died, and no one knew it," Harold said. "Legend has it that he returns to the store every now and then to keep his business going. People clean up the store before they leave. The next day, there are groceries lined up on the aisle shelf, waiting to be bagged. This happens once a month. The gentleman made his presence known to the new owner, a lady. The previous owner had an idea who it was." The members sat in the store for three days, but the only thing they captured on video was particles flying through the air when the air conditioner was turned on. Harold drove up on the last day of the investigation to give the group a hand and discovered that some boys were outside of the store yelling through the vents. "We had to discard all of the evidence we had collected because we did not know about the kids next door yelling through the vents in the air conditioning making the EVPs. We were really disappointed because we were hoping to find the groceries stacked up on the shelf," Harold said.

Not all of the evidence collected by the Bangor Ghost Hunters Association is fake. During one investigation, the group captured the striking image of a child's head coming through a wall. "It looked like it was a young boy," Harold said. "The head came through the wall, looked at the cameraman, and went back through the wall. The cameraman said he saw something in the viewfinder, but it was too small. When he brought it up on the big TV monitor we have here, we saw what he saw. It happened so quickly that we had to slow it down, but we saw what he saw. The child's head was translucent, which really took us by surprise." This photograph is also significant because it is the only thing Harold has ever photographed that he actually saw through a viewfinder.

Bangor Ghost Hunters has a case at a local school that has been going on for a year. "They have shown us some incredible videos and photographs, but we weren't there to witness it, like a Pepsi can flying off the computer desk,' Harold said. "Being a magician, I somewhat duplicated it. But I have not found any proof that they are doing the same thing. They want to keep it confidential. This does not mean I trust them more, though. During my interview with the staff, a teacher spoke up and repeated exactly what the other teacher had experienced, so she is backing up a story she didn't experience. This is why I think the power of suggestion is at work here." So far, the group has been unable to investigate the school because one very religious school board member is afraid that if Harold's group goes into the school and investigates it, the wrath of God will come down on everyone connected with the school. "We respect people's religious beliefs and we're not going to force this one lady to let us go in and do it. We hope the school board lets us investigate the school, but we are not going to force the issue," Harold said.

Of all of Harold's investigations, two stand out. One of them was conducted at a bar in Old Town, Maine. Harold was called in by the owner of the bar at 2:00 A.M. He went to the bar alone because he gave his team the night off. Harold was talking to the owner and the bartender when he felt someone's hand on his shoulder. He spun around, and no one was there. "I turned my tri-field meter on, and it went thermal. I snapped a picture, but I couldn't see what I was doing, and I caught a corner of the bar. Whatever it was disappeared. About ten minutes later, the men heard someone drop one of the big steel tables in the upper bar. They searched the bar, but everything seemed to be in place. At the time, the cameras were running, so the owner asked, 'What do you see through the infra-red?' We brought it down and hooked it up to his TV, and we picked up a spiritual voice of a woman calling the owner's name. This was accompanied by a floating ball of light." The men did not see the floating orb with the naked eye, nor had they heard anyone talking before they listened to the video. In addition, no women were present. "We could never prove it to be a hoax. The owner and his father and a few family friends identified it as the voice of his deceased mother. He got out of the bar, gave the bar back to his father, went across the street, and opened up a pawn shop,"

Harold said. Harold will always remember this case because it was his first physical encounter with an entity.

Another memorable one case was held at a cemetery in Codville, Maine: "We were videotaping. We had five members and ten other people who were family members of the client. Over the first grave, there was a 'traveler'—a ball of light. The camera picked it up. It's just going back and forth in a circle. At first we thought it was a firefly, but it didn't blink. We checked out that possibility that it was a car driving by, but there was no dirt road in that section of the woods or traffic lights. We found out later that it was a fresh grave. Someone had been buried that day, and we didn't know about it. We captured the light on video." The cameraman recorded the light for two and a half minutes. Then Harold told him to stay there for five minutes and take more video, this time to the right of the grave. The entire time he was filming, the cameraman did not see the light in the viewfinder. The next day, the group returned to the cemetery and discovered that they had been filming over a fresh grave.

During special times of the year, like Halloween, the Bangor Ghost Hunters Association takes reporters to the Jackson Cemetery in Myra, Maine. "We take reporters out there because we have gotten a lot of stuff out there. It's the most active cemetery we know of," Joe says. Even though Harold realizes that "scary places" and "scary photographs" can garner considerable publicity for his group, he wants it made clear that so far, his group has never encountered anything that meant anybody any harm: "Most of our cases involve children and young lady spirits. They don't pose a danger to anybody, except for people who run into walls or fall down flights of stairs when they see them."

NORTH EAST PARANORMAL SOCIETY
Augusta, Maine
Stacey Badillo, Director
spiritsofmaine.tripod.com

Stacey Badillo had had experiences with ghosts growing up, but she passed them off as figments of her imagination. She finally "caught the bug" in 2000 when she found a photograph of herself and some friends and noticed, for the first time, the image of a rather ominous-looking face. "I searched the Internet for others with the same interests and joined MPRA [the Maine Paranormal Research Association]. I realized that I need to follow my own path, and NEPS (North East Paranormal Society) was born," Stacey said. "I feel I am gifted with clairvoyant abilities, which I am trying to develop." Stacey's codirector, Scott Russell, has been enthralled with the unexplained and everything paranormal all his life: " I have had many experiences, from harmless playful spirit activity to being visited by my grandmother after she crossed over to assure me that she was OK and I was going to be OK too. I was eight years old at the time. I have also witnessed strange phenomena during overnight stays in graveyards. I have taken photographs and upon developing them, found strange things that weren't there when I snapped the pictures." Nineteen-year-old researcher Casey Braley has also had a lifelong interest in the paranormal. "By the time I was eight, I could feel, hear, and see things that most would think were impossible," Casey said. "Most would call this 'the sixth sense,' which happens to run through my family from my mother's side." Because Casey had never really experienced genuine fear, he decided at the age of twelve that he was going to become a paranormal investigator some day.

Part of the mission of the North East Paranormal Society is to prove the continuity of life by providing scientific gathered through research and personal experiences. Because two of the members of the group are sensitive, to some extent, they employ both a scientific and a metaphysical approach to investigating. The group's equipment list includes the standard scientific equipment, such as

scientific what

digital cameras, microcassette recorders, infrared thermometer, and video camera recorders. However, the members also bring along holy water blessed by the Catholic Church, prayers, rosaries, sea salt, and sage smudges. Stacey also conducts seances as a form of spirit communication during investigations, but she refuses to use Ouija boards, which she, like so many investigators, considers to be dangerous. Stacey uses her psychic abilities to determine when the group takes pictures and where the EVP recorders and surveillance cameras should be set up. Once the paranormal phenomena have been validated, the group cleanses the site and performs spiritual cleansing for the homeowners. The group also assists earthbound entities with crossing over.

Another part of the group's mission is to educate and help the public. For this reason, Stacey prefers to investigate private residences: "In a private home, I get to know the clients in person, not just what's written in history books about them. For a day, a night, a week, maybe even longer, I get to be a part of these people's lives and to maybe make a difference in how they sleep at night or how they cope with the death of a loved one. In some ways, I feel like I make a difference."

The North East Paranormal Society begins each investigation by asking questions regarding the history of the buildings, the land, or the family in order to form a basis for an investigation. "Gathering information is as important to an investigation as the investigation itself," Stacey says. Because many children have an inborn sensitivity to the presence of spirits, Stacey has prepared a separate list of questions for them, such as, "Do you have a 'friend' that you see and hear in your house?" "Has your 'friend' ever broken anything?" "Does your 'friend' tell you bad things?" "What does your 'friend' look like?" "Where do you usually see your 'friend'?" "Do you know your 'friend's' name? "Is your 'friend' a child or adult?"

The group's most memorable investigation was conducted from August through October of 2002 in Androscoggin County, Maine. NEPS was called in on a case involving a school that was being built on property where a haunted farmhouse was standing. "Due to the size of the property, we called in our mentors from TAPS to

assist us in a cleansing of the property," Stacey said." "Carl Johnson taught me a great deal about prayers to use during my cases,
and I found myself following him around, asking questions." In
the course of the investigation, Stacey decided to knock on one of
the abandoned farmhouse's doors in the hope that someone—or
something—would knock back. To her delight, all of the members
heard a knocking resound from inside the farmhouse. One member,
however, was not happy to hear the spectral sound. "She screamed
and ran, trying to get out of the entryway," Stacey said. "I had to
push a screen door open so she could get out, and when we finally
all got back to the driveway, she had calmed down somewhat and
insisted that she hadn't been the one screaming." Stacey had to
play the voice recorder back for the young woman to convince her
that she indeed was the one screaming. Stacey says that this is one
of her favorite investigations because she had the opportunity to
work with Carl Johnson, a man whom she greatly admires. She
is also proud of the evidence that her group collected that night.
"NEPS got a few neat pictures of possible apparitions moving on
the stairwell of the old farmhouse," Stacey said.

Stacey has been on investigations where the fear in the air was
almost palpable. One of her members became so frightened that
she had a panic attack on-site and had to resign from the group.
Stacey had a similar experience on a different investigation, but
her reaction was far different from the other young lady's: "I was
on one case that I am pretty sure was 'bad' [i.e., demonic]. I was
growled at by an unseen force while standing at the top of the
stairs. I also had the feeling that someone or something wanted
to push me down the stairs. I calmly left the area [instead of running away]." Stacey is uncomfortable in the presence of demons,
primarily because she does not believe she has the expertise to deal
with them. As a rule, she refers these homeowners to Carl Johnson
of New England Anomalies Research or Jim Petrino of Skeleton
Crew Paranormal Research.

NEPS is a very high-profile group, having been featured in psychic fairs, parades, city functions, and news stories in newspapers
and magazines. "I also leave business cards, bookmarks, and fli-
ers in stores and in towns that I visit," Stacey said. She also has

one license plate that says GHOSTS and another that says GOSTGRL. Interestingly enough, all of this exposure has not brought the group into conflict with the religious community. "We have not received a lot of criticism because there are more and more people who are open to the spirit world," Stacey says. "My church just wishes that I take precautions on my investigations, but that's about it."

MAINE SUPERNATURAL
Bucksport, Maine
Emeric Spooner, Director
mysite.verizon.net/vzeqnk8x

Librarian Emeric Spooner has been interested in the supernatural ever since he first realized that he was sharing the bedroom in his boyhood home with a ghost: "As a child, I slept in a room with a closet that opened by itself. The closet used to be a back stairwell. I had a bureau with drawers that pulled out, and I pulled out the drawers every night in front of the door to keep it from opening. Years later, a new owner had a daughter who slept in my old room. She asked my mother if we ever heard or saw anything because her daughter claimed that a little girl came out of her closet and played with her at night." Other family members also claimed to have seen a little ten-year-old girl in a long white dress walking in the house and on the grounds. Emeric has heard doors slam, windows shut, and knocking sounds in other parts of the house when no one else was around.

Emeric founded Maine Supernatural in 2004. The only other full-time investigator is his mother. The group has four part-time members, including a retired married couple who are friends of Emeric's. Emeric believes that his mother, who was born with a cowl over her face, imbued him with some of the psychic abilities that she has had all of her life: "She is able to sense spirits. I have 'trace senses undeveloped.' This means that if I concentrate really hard at a grave site or a historical location, I can barely envision the person we are there to see. I have done it successfully three times, backed up with photos and EVPs of what I saw, after I saw them."

It was this sensitivity to the spirit world that enabled Emeric to tap into the emotions emanating from the house he grew up in.

The primary mission of Maine Supernatural is to get certifiable proof of life after death. Because many historical sites are reputed to be haunted, it is often easier to gather evidence at an old inn or mansion than at a private residence that may or may not be haunted. "Historical places are a favorite because they are readily available and can be revisited numerous times. The evidence is there for the taking," Emeric says. For these reasons, Maine Supernatural has investigated sixteen private residences and well over a hundred historic sites. One of his favorite historic sites is the foundation of a hotel that burned down in 1898. "Every time we run an investigation there, we get EVPs and photos," Emeric says.

After investigating a site, Emeric usually spends up to two days examining the evidence in the evidence lab in his basement. "My evidence lab consists of my computer headphones and speakers that I use to process photographs and EVPs," Emeric says. He describes the approach his group takes to paranormal investigating as "old school" because his members do not use high-tech equipment like night vision cameras and temperature guns. For the most part, Maine Supernatural collects evidence by using digital cameras and digital voice recorders. Only 10 percent of Emeric's investigations reveal genuine hauntings, based primarily on personal experiences and feelings.

EVPs, in Emeric's opinion, are much more meaningful than orbs. "I have never seen [an orb] that couldn't be explained as either dust or moisture," Emeric says. "EVPs, on the other hand, are the only unexplainable evidence that can be obtained with any certifiable proof and then shown to other people." Emeric has found that 95 percent of all spirit photography can be explained away, but only 80 percent of EVPs have a logical explanation. "If you have a voice that is not yours on a recording, and you can't make it out, and you play it in reverse, and the words are clear, how can such evidence be fabricated?" Emeric asks. One of the most disturbing of all the EVPs Emeric has recorded is a collection of three voices that scream, in unison, "I can hear us." Emeric refers to this particular phenomenon as "multivoice."

Like most veteran paranormal investigators, Emeric has had some encounters with the supernatural that have been a little too close for comfort: "I have had batteries drained that were fully charged. Once when my back was turned, a book flew across the room and landed sixteen feet from the shelf it was resting on. We were in a three-story mansion one time, and a door forcefully slammed shut. There was no breeze or draft in the house at that time."

Emeric finds out about some historic sites by reading "true crime" books about historical murders. One of his favorite investigations was conducted at the site of the Trim murders. On October 13, 1876, a fire completely gutted the barn and carriage house of the Trim homestead. Neighbors searching through the smoldering ruins found the burned corpse of seventy-four-year-old Robert Trim in the carriage house. His arms and legs had been completely burned away. Moving to the remains of the barn, searchers found the charred skeleton of Robert Trim's daughter, Mrs. Melissa Thayer. Her body was in the same condition as her father's. Mrs. Thayer's four-year-old daughter, who had been staying with her mother at the Trim homestead, was never found. A sailor named Captain Smith was found guilty of murder and sentenced to life in prison. He died thirty years later, in 1908, after being struck in the head with a pipe by a fellow inmate.

On October 13, 2006, 130 years after the Trim family was murdered, Maine Supernatural investigated the burned-out foundation of the home of Robert Trim and his family. By 6:30 P.M., Emeric had taken more than fifty photographs at the site. Suddenly, his co-investigator claimed that her voice recorder was knocked out of her hand into a ditch. However, Emeric is convinced that her hands were so cold that she simply dropped the recorder. An hour or so later, it was completely dark. "An eerie mist was starting to roll in," Emeric said. "I took one photo that captured a very distinct and impressive shadow matrix, complete with what looks like eyeglasses, a personal first, which I didn't discover until much later." While Emeric was collecting EVPs, he noticed that one of the dogs that had been barking all evening seemed to be answering his questions. "Instantly after I asked my question, a dog barked down towards Harriman's," Emeric said. "Never missing a beat, I said, 'Bark once for no, and two barks for yes.'" At this point, the dog barked twice, but was silent after that.

Maine Supernatural has been criticized over the years, but not by the religious community. "We have been criticized for attempting to add too much humor to a web site for entertainment value. Or for not giving exact locations of private residence on our web site. Or for featuring matrix photos on my site, which are nothing more than the mind's ability to make faces and shapes in a photograph. Some people believe my matrix photographs are hoaxes," Emeric says. The only criticism that has ever caused him to reconsider his approach to investigating is the charge that his group is not being scientific enough.

CENTRAL MAINE RESEARCHERS AND INVESTIGATORS OF THE PARANORMAL
Turner, Maine
Jason Porter, Director
centralmaineparanormal.com

Jason began probing the "big" questions while living in his grandfather's house. Three months after his grandmother died, he had a very strange experience with a Beta VCR. "The old Beta VCRs had an on and off switch," Jason said. "It made a clicking sound. I was sitting in my grandfather's living room three months after my grandmother had died. I was living with my grandfather. It was after school. I was just sitting there. I was getting ready to walk to the door. The VCR had not been working for a while. It was unplugged. All of a sudden, this thing clicked off and on twice. It was creepy because I could see the outlet that it was usually plugged into. Also, the 'on' light in the VCR came on."

Several years later, when Jason was a teenage Civil War reenactor, he had another bizarre experience: "I was on an island in Boston Harbor, Fort Warren. It held Confederate prisoners during the Civil War. I was sitting in a very, very big room. There was absolutely no way light could get in there. It was pitch black. There was nobody around. I was in there by myself, trying to cool off. It was very, very cool in there, about forty degrees cooler than it was in the rest of the fort. It was eleven o'clock at night. I was standing in the middle of the room with my flashlight turned off so I could adjust to the darkness. Over on one side of the room was a glowing mist. It kind of moved around one area of the room. It did it for ten seconds. I took off like a shot!" Jason credits his lack of courage to the fact that he was only fifteen years old at the time. This was the last time that he allowed fear to override his natural curiosity.

Until Jason saw the plumbers on *Ghost Hunters* conduct paranormal investigations in New England homes, he had thought of ghost hunters as scientists, college professors, or wealthy people. *Ghost Hunters* showed Jason that ordinary people are capable of exploring extraordinary phenomena. After reading books on the topic and talking to other groups across the country, Jason and his cousin, who had also had a paranormal experience, began investigating on their own. Because Jason had a good job, he was able to purchase state-of-the-art equipment. Their first investigations were conducted in the immediate area. "His house is supposedly haunted, but I never found anything there. We did a little there, and we did a relative's house. We investigated the homes of people we knew. We did graveyards and places like that. We did some investigations with another group up here at a graveyard, and we watched how they do things," Jason said.

Jason founded Central Maine Researchers and Investigators of the Paranormal in 2006. "Right now I have thirteen people in my group," Jason said. "My tech manager, my cofounder, and I all work for a hazardous waste company. One of our guys works at a home for disturbed children who can't live with their parents because they are too rowdy. We have one gentleman who is a firefighter and EMT [emergency medical technician]. We have another man who is a retired machinist. One guy works for a printing company. I have one who is on disability, but she was a housemaid. A couple more are in retail." The one quality that all the members share, besides a love of investigating, is their skepticism. "Our group sets out to prove that it's not paranormal first. We want to debug it first," Jason said. By way of "jump-starting the group," Jason arranged for Central Maine Researchers and Investigators to become a part of the TAPS family. Within a matter of weeks, the group received calls from private homes in Maine and New Hampshire. "I am very proud to be a member of the TAPS family," Jason said.

The mission of Central Maine Researchers and Investigators of the Paranormal is threefold: to help people and to possibly help any spirits or ghosts, to educate people, and to prove the existence of something that cannot be seen. Proving the existence of the paranormal is in the top ten, but it is not the most important reason for doing what he does. "First and foremost, we are there to help people," Jason said. "People call us up and say, 'Hey, I've got this going on in my house. What can I do? Come take a look.'" Because the group's primary goal is to help people, the majority of the group's cases are private residences. Jason cites as an example a case involving a couple who had completely different views toward the uncanny activity in their home: "The guy wasn't afraid of what was going on in his house, but his girlfriend was. We went in there and pretty much debunked what was going on. The young woman thought that there was demonic activity going on in the house because she was scratched, but we proved that the scratch came from a furniture staple. She was very relieved. He was kind of, 'Yeah, I told you that.'" In a case like this, Jason and his group served as a third party whose unbiased attitude toward the phenomena helped to diffuse the situation.

For Jason, collecting evidence involves more than simply turning on a meter or a recorder. Eliminating every other possible cause of the phenomenon is also part of the process, especially when recording EVPs. "EVPs could emanate from radio or CDs or ham radio," Jason said. "If you do your research beforehand and look around the area and make sure there are no CDs or radios playing, you can put more stock in your EVPs, especially if they answer a question during a conversation." Jason recorded a startling EVP while conducting an investigation in a very small house in New Hampshire. "It took five steps from the kitchen to walk down the hall to the living room," Jason said. "We were taking a break at two o'clock in the morning. We were having coffee, and I made the comment, 'By the end of the night, we're going to be on a sugar high, and we'll be running all over the place, like a gerbil on crack.' And a voice came in on an EVP that said, 'I don't think so.' It's so clear. My tech manager was there too. He's very skeptical. He said there were no other voices in the house, no CB antennas. It was two A.M. There was nobody driving by with a CB antenna." Jason became even more excited when he discovered that a second recorder had also recorded the voice: "We had one recorder upstairs with an external microphone and one in the kitchen. The entity was in the room with us, but because the house was so tiny, the recorder upstairs picked it up too." Later on that evening, Jason was sitting in the living room talking to one of his investigators when, once again, he recorded an EVP. Neither time did his group collect any corroborative evidence.

Jason has a theory as to why ghosts often make an appearance when the investigators are unprepared: "My opinion on it is that ghosts are people. If a person were shy when he was alive, wouldn't he be shy in death? If you were trying to coax somebody to talk who is shy, the person would probably be reluctant to speak up. But if you are just having a random conversation with someone else, it's easier for him to jump in on the conversation than to actively engage them in a conversation. So it actually makes sense, in a way. This is why you get more evidence when you aren't looking for it."

Jason has never photographed a full-bodied apparition, but he did take a picture of a soldier sitting in the basement of Cedar Creek Battlefield. "If you know anything about Civil War soldiers, you can point out specific things on his uniform," Jason says. "You might not see it. I see it. We see photos of full-bodied apparitions all the time. I could do the same thing on a simple computer program. It's very hard to prove." Jason has posted the photograph on his web site, even though he knows that not everyone will be able to make out the figure of the soldier.

In order to make personal experiences in a haunted location more acceptable as evidence, Jason's investigators always work in pairs. "If you see an apparition when you're alone, you can't prove it to anybody, but if you have a witness with you who sees the same thing, you at least have another person who can collaborate your evidence. One of the rules of our group is that if you see something or hear something, don't talk to each other about it. Keep your mouth shut. Finish your investigation and back out of the room." Jason then talks to each team member separately and compares their stories to see if they match. He always separates the investigators because of the power of suggestion: "If I told you I saw the apparition of a little girl wearing a blue dress, and you saw the apparition too, but you weren't sure if it was a blue dress—you thought it might have been pink—then you'll say, 'Yeah, it was blue.'"

The "buddy system" also prevents Jason's investigators from becoming frightened—most of the time. "My cousin got really frightened once," Jason said. "We were visiting a local historical museum. He was in one of the rooms, and he got touched on the neck. He took off like a flash. It was almost like a replay of Brian Hernois on *Ghost Hunters*. He didn't say, 'Let's run!' He said, 'Holy s____!'" When he was half way down the stairs, Jason stopped him and told him to get back upstairs and continue the investigation. To prevent incidents like this, Jason begins every investigation by telling his members, "If you feel something, if you get touched, if you hear or see something, do not—DO NOT—run! If the client's around, you don't want him to see you get extremely frightened. The next thing you know, they're moving out of the house. You don't want them running and tripping over stuff because there are a lot of wires lying around. When you're running at full speed, you never know what you're going to hit. You don't run away from a situation. Take a deep breath, turn, and walk out."

Jason's most memorable investigation occurred just a few weeks before this interview. One night, he received a telephone call from a man who said he was experiencing some intense paranormal activity in his house. He had even captured some of the disturbances on video. "We drove three hours north and spent two nights there," Jason said. "On one video, you can see an object on a shelf. Then in the next millisecond, it's on the floor. You couldn't see it fall. He said you couldn't capture it in midair. I asked the guy what kind of equipment he was using. He was using a VCR that recorded it thirty frames per second. He challenged me. He said there is no way you can capture something in midair at thirty frames per second. I said, 'I don't believe you.' I walked out of the room." At three o'clock in the afternoon, Jason accepted the man's challenge. He changed the speed of his video camera to thirty frames per second. Then he asked his tech manager to walk upstairs with a Gatorade bottle full of water and drop it. "Lo and behold, you can watch it fall from his hand," Jason said. "You can watch it fall to the floor. It even bounced a couple of times. I had him do it twice, and I recorded it both times. Then I asked the homeowner to come in. He got quite upset. He didn't yell or scream, but you could tell he was agitated. He pretty much left us alone for the rest of the night. I talked to another group that had been up there, and they said when they were there, they just let him ramble on. He would not leave them alone, so I must have ticked him off. All I did was prove a point to him. I wasn't being a jerk or anything. Come to find out, the guy was a little bit off his rocker."

Actually, Jason was surprised by the man's erratic behavior because the group had interviewed him on the telephone for an hour beforehand: "I'm pretty good at judging character, so I can usually figure out if somebody is OK within an hour. This guy fooled me, though. On the phone, he's a completely different person, quiet and reserved. He answered questions in a very short, abrupt way, but when you meet him in person, he won't stop babbling." Jason was particularly taken aback by a statement the man made not long after the group arrived: "I want to bottle up the ghost, put him in a cage, and get people to pay me money to see my ghost."

Unlike most investigators, Jason's penchant for ghost hunting occasionally conflicts with a second obsession of his—Civil War reenacting. "I was born in Massachusetts, raised in New Hampshire, lived in New England all my life, but I'm a Confederate reenactor. I've been a Confederate reenactor for ten years. I'm a member of the 29th Georgia. All my relatives fought for the Federal Army. When people ask why I do this, I explain, 'Well, the Yanks need someone to shoot at.'"

MASSACHUSETTS

SPIRIT ENCOUNTER RESEARCH TEAM

Chicopee, Massachusetts
Rob Tremblay, Director
Rick Boifvere, Co-Director
sertma.tripod.com

Rob Tremblay became interested in the paranormal through past personal experiences. Like so many founders of paranormal research groups, Rob lived in a haunted house. Growing up, he became accustomed to objects moving on their own. He also took some startling spirit photographs in his house. However, an intensely personal loss really sparked his curiosity about the unknown: "My mom passed in 2000," Rob said. "She knew how I would handle things when it was time for her to go. The last time we were asked to leave the room when she was in ICU, I was thinking, 'Things are OK. I'm going to get back to see her again.' All night, we went in to see her and went back to the waiting room. The last time I went to the waiting area, I felt her hand on my back. I think it was her way of letting me know she might be gone but she's still here." Rob started his group four years after she died.

A year after the Spirit Encounter Research Team got started, Rob's co-director, Rick Boifvere, joined the group. "My mother is a practicing professional medium and has been for twenty-five to thirty years," Rick said. "She always told me it was something I would be doing at some point in my life, and I didn't believe her. Then about twelve years ago, I got sick and began questioning my mortality because I was afraid I wasn't going to pull through. I decided after that to go to the local spiritualist church. I met up with a young minister there whom I'm still with." Not only has Rick been doing private one-on-one readings for about nine years, but he also conducts services in a half-dozen churches in the New England area. He would like to "branch out" some day and help others tap into their latent psychic abilities. "Some people might be communicators, like me," Rick said. "Some people might be healers. We all have the same abilities. Whether we choose to develop them or not is up to us."

Rick says that some of the members of the Spiritualist church are interested in joining up or in giving the information regarding places where we can go on investigations. "For the most part, the people who go to the Spiritualist Church are very open to [the paranormal]," Rick says. "They understand that the reason I am doing this is to get knowledge to more people. They realize that this isn't anything strange or weird or anything to be afraid of, that this is just a natural part of our lives and that we have kind of just pushed it away through our society and through whatever teachings we've encountered."

Rick's belief that the spirits are everywhere has made it difficult for him to tell clients that their house is not haunted: "When I debunk a haunting, I try to explain to the clients exactly what is happening. I figure that wherever I go, I'm going to pick up something, whether it is something that is affecting the physical worlds or not. The spirit world is all around us, so I wouldn't be able to go into a house and say, 'There's nobody here and there's nothing here spiritually.' I could answer questions about things that are happening that are affecting people, but there wouldn't be a house where there's no activity at all because I would pick up activity, even if nobody else did."

The group's mission is to acquire information and to help other people. Although the group has collected some significant evidence, Rob does not believe that any of it amounts to indisputable proof of the existence of the paranormal. At some point someone might get something that is extremely significant. "That's the Holy Grail of what we're looking for," Rob says, "but at this time we're just looking for information to share with others who have the same interests. People have been trying to prove the existence of the paranormal for centuries, so I'm not sure what the chances are of that happening. It's kind of a back-burner issue right now. We just want to get as much information and photographs."

The Spirit Encounter Research Team collects evidence using the scientific and the metaphysical methods. "We're on the low side of financial funding, so we just have the basics," Rob says. "We use

EMF recorders and digital and magnetic recorders, remote cameras, and Polaroid cameras. We don't have anything that's highly
technical or expensive at this point." Of the metaphysical tools
at their disposal, the members do not use dowsing rods or Ouija
boards, which Rick views as the door to hell: "It's like leaving the
door open, and anybody can come in if you don't know what you're
doing. There's a rule in the Spiritualist church that 'like attracts
like.' If you were sitting around with a bunch of monks who are
using a Ouija board, they're going to get that positive energy. But
if it's a bunch of drunk teenagers playing with it, they're going to
get lower level energy that might be harmful."

Rick himself is the team's primary metaphysical tool. He prefers to go into an investigation without knowing who lived on the
property before. "I prefer to be kept in the dark," Rick says. "Then
afterwards, I tell them what I got, and they see if it corresponds to
the history of the place. The vibes I get usually fit into the history.
I might get things that no one knows about, but I might also get
things that are a matter of record. The only thing I want to know
is where the activity is, so that I do not waste my time in the cellar when the activity is in the attic. I also want to know what type
of activity [has been reported] so that if something is going to be
thrown at me, I'll know that before I walk into a room. I try to be
a part of the investigation and yet not a part of it." Rick tells the
other members where he feels the activity is centrally located so
they will know where to set up the cameras and recorders. Sometimes, the group sends Rick into a house by himself to see if he
can determine what is going on by giving the clients a reading. At
the present time, Rick is the only member of the group who is a
medium. "Rob and his wife are both sensitive but not developed at
this point. They are more involved in running the group and setting up the technology," Rick says.

Orbs are much less significant than EVPs, from Rob and Rick's
point of view. Both agree that orbs are probably dust, moisture,
smoke, insects, or lens refraction. "Sometimes in video footage,
they look like they interact with us, but so does dust with static
electricity, and so do insects," Rick says. "So unless orbs are overtly
intelligent, I'm not going to put much stock in them." Some of the

EVPs the group has collected, on the other hand, have been very impressive. During an investigation at a cemetery, Rob recorded a little girl who said, "Rob, talk to me!" and "Rob, over here."

The Spirit Encounter Research Team publicizes itself primarily through word of mouth and business cards. "One time we were at a restaurant, and we overheard people talking about weird things that were happening at their house, like lights turning on and off and things moving," Rick said. "We interrupted them and told them what we do and gave them business cards." So far, the group has not done any television programs or interviews with the media, but it will be featured in a documentary called *Fourteen Degrees* that is being produced by New Gravity Media. Rick explained the title: "In the middle of the summer, it was eighty-five degrees in a room. It was un-air-conditioned. And yet, they found one cold spot that was only fourteen degrees. There was no AC or vents in the area. There was no way to explain the fourteen degree cold spot."

So far, the group has not encountered a demonic entity. Rick believes the group is protected from negative forces "because of our ordination and because of the fact that we have reverence and respect for what we are doing. I feel that if we are putting out positive energy, we will get back positive energy. I bring a sense of humor with me, and even though some clients have been offended by it, I feel that it's protective energy and that it creates a protective bubble around us. I feel that people in the spirit world are still people and that they still have a sense of humor. I feel that if people are 'high' spirits, they will come out a little bit better and connect with me a little bit stronger." Rick admits that the group has visited a few sites that he felt did not emit "positive vibes," but he would not go so far as to label them as demonic. "I don't have any fear of such things, but I couldn't tell you how I'd respond because at this point in my development, I haven't encountered anything like that," Rick said.

Right now, the group is conducting most of its investigations at inns and bed-and-breakfasts. One of these historic businesses was the Colonial House Inn in Cape Cod. "It had a very positive, family-oriented feel to it," Rick said. "They gave us the run of the place. We set up a recorder in a tower. It was such an old building that if anyone were to walk up the stairs, the entire building would creak and moan, so no one could have gotten past us when we were sleeping downstairs. In the morning there were children's voices on the recorder, children that had run up the stairs. They were laughing and yelling and running back down the stairs. Obviously, that is something we would not have missed if it had happened to us physically. But it was a very, very positive feeling." Rick says that everyone on the team was either touched, pinched, or pushed, but in a playful way. While the group was there, Rick did a reading for the owner. "He had tears in his eyes when I told him about some of the people who were around him, and he recognized who they were. It was a very positive experience and probably the best investigation I have been on. I didn't feel any fear in anybody," Rick said.

Rob had his most memorable investigation when the group was first starting out: "My wife and I were brought out to a case in Maine by another group. After investigating this one area where I thought I saw something, I came to the conclusion that it was the silhouette of an apparition. We were wrapping everything up, and there was this door with a window and a light on the other side. The hallway went straight back four or five feet. I opened up the door into a kitchen, which went across, almost like a 'T.' The image that I saw was that of a man walking on the other side of the door from the left to the right. Several of the other investigators witnessed the door open and close by itself. You had to turn the doorknob to get into it. That door was opening and closing by itself. I was excited. I wanted to go explore it." Unfortunately, Rob did not have an opportunity to photograph the apparition because by the time he entered the room, it had disappeared. He has concluded that the apparition was the ghost of a servant. "It's my understanding that that area back in the eighteen hundreds was actually used by the servants," Rob said, "and it was just the way it carried itself when I saw it going across. It was the first dead person I had ever seen, a full-body apparition. That's why this was a special case for me."

Fear has taken its toll on the group's membership over the years. One member called Rob one morning to say that she was not going to be in the group anymore, following a cemetery investigation. "I remember she was kind of scared, and I think [the cemetery] was too overwhelming for her. I do not know of anything that happened that would have frightened her. She never really explained, but you could tell she was scared while she was there. It's possible that she sensed something that the rest of us weren't tuned into," Rob said.

The group visits cemeteries every couple of months. The group uses them as training grounds for new members because, as a rule, evidence is pretty easy to collect at cemeteries. "We've gotten some weird pictures like light anomalies there, and, of course, orbs," Rob said, "which really aren't that impressive. We even photographed the full-body apparition of a woman at a cemetery. I normally show the picture around to a few people and ask them 'What do you think you see in this picture?' They usually go, like, 'Is that a ghost?' and I say, 'You tell me. Does it look like a ghost to you?' When I showed it to T. J. Tucker, the director of W.R.A.I.T.H., his response was 'Oh, my God! Oh, my God!'" Rob has not posted the photograph on his web site because he worries about people claiming it as their own.

Spirit Encounter Research Team differs from many groups in that it does not operate independently of other groups in the area. "We pretty much work hand in hand with T. J. Tucker's team, W.R.A.I.T.H.," Rob says. "They'll ask us to come in and help out with their cases, and they'll come in and help us with ours. We normally work together in a space where we have room for more than one group. If we're short-staffed, we might ask W.R.A.I.T.H. for one or two people, and they've done the same with us. If it's their case, then we'll turn the evidence over to them. They'll turn it over to us if it's our case." If all groups were as willing to share evidence as the Spirit Encounter Research Team and W.R.A.I.T.H. are, some real progress might be made in the field of paranormal investigation.

W.R.A.I.T.H.
Worcester, Massachusetts
T. J. Tucker, Director
www.myspace.com/w_r_a_i_t_h

T J. Tucker became interested in the paranormal because he has had experiences with things that made him wonder, "OK. What the heck was that?" One of his family photos had outlines of people who weren't really there. "We were getting a lot of circles on photos that we couldn't understand," T.J. said. "They weren't like orb photos. These almost looked like water spots on the film." In 1989, T.J. and his younger brother witnessed a shadow person coming at them from his brother's room. "It walked down the hallway and through the doorway without opening the door. That freaked us out. We were just sitting there, half-awake and half-asleep," T.J. said. At the time, he was sixteen years old.

The original group was started in 1995/1996. "Our current group is a different form of that group," T.J. says. "This group was restructured about two years ago." W.R.A.I.T.H. now has about twenty members, including several stay-at-home moms and a nurse. T.J. is a student. Most of the people in his group have had paranormal experiences. "They have learned to deal with it and accept it as part of their lives," T.J. says. "The house I live in is haunted. I'm used to it." The other team members either live in places that are haunted or experience things so frequently that it's no big deal to them anymore.

The group's purpose is to prove the existence of ghosts scientifically. "We go through and exhaust every single possible theory," T.J. says. "Then once we exclude everything, we can consider it possibly paranormal. The other part of our mission statement is to help other people. For a lot of people, their initial reaction is fear. We help them control their fear and to retake control of their house. We show them that if you fear these things, it just gives them more power. We tell them to be firm [with the spirits] and tell them, 'This is my house. You don't belong here. You need to move on.'"

Although W.R.A.I.T.H. promotes itself as a science-based group, T.J. admits that his members do use their innate psychic abilities: "I can see and hear them. The other cofounder can speak to them. It's really weird because it seems that every time she carries a voice recorder, she's the one getting the EVPs. They're all coming to her because they want to talk to her." T.J.'s cofounder made extremely close contact with one of these spirits during an investigation of a cemetery where a couple of ministers were buried. As she was passing by one particular grave, she could feel something on her back. "She said it felt like she was giving somebody a piggyback ride," T.J. said. "She kept screaming, 'There's something on my back! There's something on my back!'" The other team W.R.A.I.T.H. was with that night had a wiccan with them, and she tried doing a couple of spells to get it off. The two cofounders of the other team were ministers. They tried blessing her, but the entity just wouldn't go away until the teams left the cemetery.

The next week, W.R.A.I.T.H.'s cofounder played back the tape she had made with the digital recorder she had brought with her. T.J. said, "It sounded like a broadcast of a Southern Baptist preacher. The guy who was buried in this grave that she passed was a Southern Baptist preacher who preached in this particular town. It sounds like a radio broadcast that we captured on that tape, but the area we were in is a known dead zone. It's an almost crystal-clear preacher giving a sermon the entire time we were in the cemetery. The thing is, there's no cellular services. There's hardly any television or radio reception either. The closest tower for any kind of broadcast is about three towns over." The recording of the EVP stopped as soon as she walked over the cemetery wall. This was about the same time that she said, "I don't have anything on my back anymore."

T.J.'s cofounder had a similar experience in a different graveyard. "This spirit was not happy that she was taking pictures of his tombstone, and he started cursing her, saying, 'I'm getting pissed! I'm getting pissed! Please, no more photos.'" Then he started cursing," T.J. said. Once again she was the only person on the team to whom the spirits seemed to be drawn.

T.J. has encountered maybe two genuine demonic entities in all the years that he has been investigating, in addition to several spirits that were unhappy that they were there. "They were downright nasty," T.J. said. "They tried to manipulate me and the other person who was there. You have to be careful with them because they will try to get you to believe in something that they want you to believe or do." To protect himself against demons such as these, when he goes on investigations T.J. wears crystals and religious symbols that have been blessed by the Catholic Church and by friends who are witches. T.J. believes that these charms actually work: "One of the times that I actually did encounter a demonic entity, I had a pendant that basically looked like a cross. It had a piece of crystal that went down and two pieces on the side and then a small one on the top. The two on the side and the one on the top burst. All that was left was that one crystal hanging down. This was definitely a demonic entity. After it burst, we just got out there." The first time T.J. made the acquaintance of a demon, he and a friend were investigating a site outside of Boston. "We had just the basic equipment, and we went to places where we heard stuff was going on," T.J. said. "We were very firm with it. We told it, 'If you're doing stuff like that, we're leaving.' It got mad, and we just ignored it and moved on."

Of all the evidence that T.J. has collected, he believes that EVPs are the best, but even EVPs cannot be accepted as indisputable scientific proof by themselves: "As I have told many people, EVPs can be many things. They can be stray broadcasts. They could be CB radio. But if you've got a photo or EMF fluctuations or more than one radiation collection, that gives EVPs more validity. This makes people think, 'That's got to be something, then.'" Orbs, on the other hand, are much less reliable. "Ninety-nine percent of orbs are dust, moisture, or bugs," T.J. said. "The invention of the digital camera has made it even worse. A lot people don't understand how digital cameras work. If you get a little piece of dust when the flash is going off, a digital camera is going to make it look like an orb."

Capturing photographic anomalies is also important to the members of W.R.A.I.T.H. One of the group's most startling photographs was taken on a residential case. "There's this room that's closed off, but we kept hearing sounds coming from inside, so we decided to go in there, just to see if there were any animals that had been trapped in there," T.J. said. "We waited half a minute after the door was open until things had settled down. Then we went into the room, checked it out, and snapped the picture. When we went downstairs, we checked out the photo, and it looks like the head of somebody, the head and shoulders of a female. You can make out the definition in the face. You can see hair coming off the sides. It's a black-and-white photo. Everyone we have shown it to has said, 'Oh, my God!'"

Half of W.R.A.I.T.H.'s investigation are historic sites, and the other half are private residences. "We work very closely with a group from Chicopee called SERT [Spirit Encounter Resarch Team] Paranormal," T.J. says. "They do a lot of bed-and-breakfasts. We'll go with them from time to time when they need extra manpower, and sometimes, we go to bed-and-breakfasts. For every house we investigate, we do a historic site." W.R.A.I.T.H. has relationships with a few towns and historic sites and, as a result, has no trouble getting access to these places. However, the group has had trouble getting permission to investigate a few historic sites, due in large part to the antics of amateur ghost hunters. "Kids who have been trespassing at places like cemeteries on the pretence that they are ghost hunting have ruined it for the rest of us by vandalizing and knocking over and spray painting tombstones. No matter what the site is, we go through the proper channels to get permission. And we don't just get permission from the land's owner. We have contacted the local police department and tried to clear it by them as well," T.J. said. One site that is currently off limits to ghost hunters is a cemetery located behind an airport. It is considered to be on Worcester Airport property because some of the landing lights and a power station are located out there. "Ever since 9/11, you can't get permission [from the airport] to go out there," T.J. says. "It used to be that you could park back there on an access road. But after 9/11, as soon as you park there, the control tower can see you, and they can have airport security out there in minutes. I told [a paranormal investigator], 'You're going to have a hard time. You might as well give up on that site.'"

One of T.J.'s most interesting investigations was conducted at the John Stone Inn in Ashland. "It was just a friend of mine and I who went to the inn. There's a legend that John Stone haunts it and that the guy that he killed haunts it, but there's also a little girl who passed away there," T.J. said. "We both experienced the spirit of the little girl. She was basically wanting to play with us. She kept popping up everywhere we went. We were, like, 'OK, we can't play with you now.' But she was persistent. She kept trying to joke with us and to get us to play with her."

Another memorable investigation was conducted during the daytime at a local cemetery. T.J. and his cofounder were accompanied by the two cofounders of SERT Paranormal. T.J. said, "The cofounders of SERT were showing us this particular site, and we were going to do a joint investigation. The other cofounder of W.R.A.I.T.H. was being cursed at by this spirit while she was taking photos. One of the cofounders of SERT got held back. He couldn't move. It's a real interesting cemetery, and to get this much activity during the day is just amazing. I told them, 'We're definitely going to come back here at night because it is definitely going to get more interesting.'" When the researchers examined the evidence on site, they were pleased to find their cameras had caught a couple of anomalies. "This is the first time we have looked at the photos taken at a cemetery and said, 'Whoa! What is that?' We couldn't wait to get home to enhance them. We caught stuff in the background as well. The spirits were making it known that they were there."

T.J. believes that publicity is vital to the existence of a paranormal research team. Word of mouth and the Internet are probably the best forms of publicity, but W.R.A.I.T.H. has explored other avenues as well. "Robbie Thomas is a well-known psychic medium. He's making a tour of the U.S. Every stop he makes, he picks up a local group to be his home team. He picked two teams from the Boston area, but we were the first team he asked. The other group is from southern Massachusetts," T.J. says. He is trying to get the local newspaper to feature his group in an article. He is also investigating the possibility of publicizing his group with slide shows that they show in movie theaters before the movie begins. "I do all the graphic arts, so I would be able to design the advertisement myself," T.J. says. Like most groups, though, W.R.A.I.T.H. relies heavily on the positive testimony of people its members have helped, to put a positive slant on the group's endeavors.

NEW ENGLAND PARANORMAL
Chicopee, Massachusetts
Sarah Gwozdz, Co-Director
www.newenglandparanormal.com

The paranormal has always been a part of Sarah Gwozdz's life. Her uncle, who has been a ghost hunter since the 1920s, started telling her stories of his experiences when she was very young. Her interest in the field crystallized when he brought her along on a trip to Gettysburg: "While I was there, I got to talk to Mark Nesbitt. Mark loaned me some of his ghost-hunting equipment. This was the first time I ever went out on an investigation with real equipment. I was down by the spring getting my picture taken by my boyfriend and his cousins when I got an EVP of a man breathing." At the time, the rangers were getting ready to close down the park, and Sarah and her little group were the only ones present.

The membership of New England Paranormal is not as diverse as that of most New England groups. With the exception of Sarah, who works for UPS, and another member who owns a design company, most of the members of the group are police officers. "The police officers' crime detection skills help them to determine what is going on in a particular situation," Sarah says. "They are very level-headed. When we witness a phenomenon, we try to figure out what is going on, so the police officers prevent us from immediately assuming that the cause of the activity is paranormal in nature."

However, Sarah's innate skepticism does not make her immediately dismiss her clients' claims that their house is truly haunted: "When we start an investigation we always tell the homeowners, 'You're living here all the time. We are only here a couple of hours.

So if something doesn't happen while we are here, that does not mean that your house isn't haunted.'" Sarah adds that a number of her clients encourage her group to disprove the haunting because they are frightened at the thought that their house is haunted.

At the time of the interview, New England Paranormal had two hundred applications for membership. "Keeping one's cool" in potentially stressful situations is one of the primary traits Sarah looks for in a member of her team: "We try to recruit people who will be calm and professional because we are going into a situation where the [client] is scared to death. We don't want our investigators running out of their house screaming. We don't want to scare our clients by getting scared ourselves. Our main goal is to help our clients understand what is really going on, regardless of whether or not it is paranormal in origin." Even though New England Paranormal does try to screen out people who are easily frightened, Sarah says that on one investigation, a member of her group walked into a room, turned around, and walked right back out again. Apparently, the investigator's "weird feelings" about the place convinced her that something was not quite right about this particular room.

Although New England Paranormal gets a lot of attention from its web site, as most New England groups do, it has also received a boost from its connection with The Atlantic Paranormal Society (TAPS). "We're in the TAPS family," Sarah says. "When people contact TAPS, Jason and Grant tell the homeowners which group is closest to them." So far, New England Paranormal's relationship with TAPS has gone no further than public relations. "We haven't been on *Ghost Hunters* yet," Sarah says.

New England Paranormal promotes itself as being purely science based, but the members also pay close attention to any "weird feelings" they have when they are on site. Sarah says, "Someone who has been around ghosts for a while can kind of tell when something is going to happen. However, the only evidence we use is physical evidence, which means that we can't use emotional evidence." Of all the different types of physical evidence that New England Paranormal does collect, orbs and EVPs are the most fascinating. "A lot of orbs are dust particles," Sarah says, "but a true orb is a cluster of energy. The presence of orbs doesn't mean that a ghost is around, though." She has found EVPs to be much more meaningful, especially those that are not in English: "One EVP we got at a private residence was in Portuguese. Someone in the group spoke Portuguese, and he pointed out that there are different dialects of Portuguese, and this [entity] was speaking an upper-class dialect."

An investigation at a historic mansion provided Sarah and her group with some of their most unforgettable moments. "We were there with another group. The members of my group were down in the cellar, and we heard a crash upstairs," Sarah said. "We ran up the stairs and found absolutely nothing. We radioed the other group, and they said, 'Not now! We're hearing voices.' All of us ended up getting some pretty good EVPs that night." Sarah adds that while she was in the cellar, a car moved by itself.

In this particular case, the demonic was probably not involved. However, New England Paranormal has planned for the eventuality that it might encounter evil entities some day. "The director has told me that I am welcome to contact local churches [if assistance from the clergy is needed]," Sarah says. "Keith, who has appeared on the *Ghost Hunters* television show, has worked with our group on several occasions." Despite the dangers involved in cleansing a house or banishing demons, Sarah and her group are willing to take the risks involved because, as she puts it, "These are the people who need our help the most."

ISIS
Schodack Landing, New York
Dayna Winters and Patricia Gardner, Co-Directors
www.isisinvestigations.com

ISIS is unique among ghost-hunting groups in that its members do not downplay the metaphysical aspects of their investigations. Dayna Winters says that she and her co-director, Patricia Gardner, began investigating as a way of delving deeper into a field that has fascinated them for years. "We're a coven of witches," Dayna says. "Dealing with the supernatural and the spiritual is just one more step into what we already do." In fact, everyone in the group, with the exception of two members, belongs to the coven. The members use all of their psychic abilities in investigation, as well as the standard scientific equipment. "We have a clairsentient and a psychic artist, and Dayna and I pretty much do everything," Pat says.

Dayna says that ISIS members prefer to rely on their psychic abilities during their investigations because electronic equipment tends to disturb the electronic field: "Our clairsentient Justin always has his dowsing rods with him. Those are pretty much the only tools we use." The fact that many of the hauntings ISIS has investigated have been located near large bodies of water has convinced the group that water is a conduit for paranormal activity. "When you fill a cup with water, it draws the spirits to you, and it also gives them something to use for energy to manifest," Dayna says.

Dayna believes that diversity has contributed significantly to the group's success: "I am a full-time student at Russell City University. Patricia used to work in an occult store. Our psychic artist is a social worker. Our clairsentient is a hairdresser. Mark owns his own small-engine repair business, and Matthew is a student. Robin is a student at ITT [ITT Technical Institute]. Habish was a full-time financial adviser. He is now a full-time student. I think just being who they are really enhances the group." The group's investigations also run smoothly because the group gets along so well. "We're all friends, and we work well together," Dayna says. "There is not arguing or bickering. There is no ego involved either. Each member has a job, and they do their job, and they don't worry about what everyone else is doing." All prospective members of ISIS are screened before they are admitted into the group. People who have nothing to add to the group or who cannot handle a paranormal encounter are turned down. Members must also be able to handle the physical demands of investigating. "One prospective member of our group had epilepsy," Dayna says, "and we turned him away because we were afraid that he would have a seizure on site. He understood when we explained it to him." Being blunt, Dayna and Pat believe, is essential in order to make ISIS an effective group.

Dayna says that the group's mission is threefold: "First of all, our mission is to help others who have gone through paranormal experiences, because they can be very alienating. We would also like to learn as much as we can about paranormal activity. Finally, we just like what we're doing. It's interesting stuff. We've had some pretty exciting investigations." Proving the existence of the paranormal is a secondary goal, Dayna says, because her members already believe in it. Besides, Pat adds, convincing people is often a fruitless exercise: "We don't try to change skeptics' minds about what we do. If you're a skeptic, you'll always be a skeptic. If you pay attention, you can learn a great deal."

Dayna and Pat insist that their members never work alone on an investigation. "You can't be alone because if something happens to you there's no one to help you, "Dayna says. "Also, if you're alone, there is no one around to validate what you have seen. If we have an extra one, then one group has three people."

Dayna and Pat's caseload is impressive. ISIS has done a number of historic sites—most of which are in Massachusetts, Vermont, and other parts of New England, such as Naval Park and a historic home in Vermont—but mostly its investigations center around private residences. People find out about ISIS through word of mouth, flyers, pamphlets, and its web site, but media interest has really made the public aware of the group's activities. "We get lots of media coverage around Halloween," Dayna says. "We were on a popular radio station around here, FLY 92, and News Station Fox 23 when we did the Naval Park Mansion. We have been on four other radio shows as well." ISIS has also been featured on the Discovery television show *A Haunting*. "They are doing our Vermont case," Dayna says. "It's very cool."

When ISIS is on an investigation, the group pays much more attention to EVPs than to orbs. "We put more stock in EVPs," Dayna says, "because orbs can be dust or rain or reflections. Orbs don't usually count unless there's evidence that proves what's going on." The EVPs the group has captured have been much more convincing—and dramatic: "In Orange County we had [an EVP] where someone was swearing at us, telling to get back the f____ where we came from." At another site, the client's daughter had some kind of brain disease that robbed her of the ability to speak or move. After interviewing the client, the members went over to a second house that the client owned and investigated it. Dayna says, "There were three women in the basement—Pat, myself, and the owner. The EVP we got was of a child and a woman. It was a voice saying, 'Mary, Mary, watch this!' And the child's voice said, 'And it is, Mum.' Then you can hear it laughing. It was incredible." Dayna and Pat posted the EVP on their web site after having it validated by an EVP expert.

As a rule, the group plays an EVP back for the clients without telling them what they are supposed to hear. However, because the members do this all the time, they sometimes hear things that other people don't. A good example is an EVP they recorded during an investigation they conducted at a house in Schenectady owned by one of the members of the group, Justin. "When we listened to the EVP in his apartment, we heard my name mentioned four times," Dayna said. "But when we did the tape for the EVPs, it wasn't there anymore."

The group's most memorable investigation was conducted at a historic home in Vermont. While walking around the outside of the house, one of the members took a photograph under a tree of burned material that was not visible to the naked eye. Then when they were investigating one of the bedrooms inside the house, they captured the image of a woman. They also recorded an EVP that mentioned the fire under the tree. When Dayna revealed the group's findings to the owner of the house, she said, "Before you even start talking, I want you to know that we saw a woman in the bedroom, and we got a picture of a woman in a bedroom." The family decided to dig up under the tree to make a driveway, and beneath the tree, they found a burned foundation and burned clothing. "That was really cool because it confirmed our findings," Dayna said. This is the investigation that was featured in the Discovery Channel television series *A Haunting*.

ISIS recorded even more EVPs at Justin's house in Schenectady. Pat says, "In the basement of his house, we got about thirty EVPs. We got one where the entity said it wouldn't get in our machine. We also got a number of little kids, including one little kid who said, 'I want to go home.' That one breaks my heart every time I hear it." Two of the EVPs the group recorded say, "Get out! Get out!" Two other EVPs say, "How many of you are there?" and "I heard something moving in there." One of the most interesting EVPs the group captured that night—"Keep that away from us"—was probably referring to the EMF detector.

During an investigation at an apartment house in Troy, the EVP the group recorded was even more significant because it served as corroborating evidence. "We were in the basement, and it had wooden stairs in the apartment," Dayna said. "It was the only one that had access to the basement. As we were all standing around the stairs, we could see the stairs bow from the footsteps, and we could hear the footsteps creak down the stairs. We got a picture of me on the stairs, and we had sensed something on the stairs at the time. The EVP we got said, 'I'm coming down the stairs.' It was incredible."

Sometimes, the members are able to alleviate the problem before they leave. A case in point involved a very disturbing encounter Justin had at his girlfriend's house. "A succubus went after Justin one time while he was visiting his girlfriend," Dayna said. "We have no idea how it got there. She was after him big-time. He woke up and found himself in a compromising position, and he had no idea how he got there."

Sometimes, ISIS is called upon to remove a troublesome spirit from a house. Unlike most group's that perform cleansings, ISIS does not employ Christian rituals. "Exorcisims are sanctified by the church," Dayna said. "We do banishings, which are rituals to banish anything negative from the house. These are wiccan cleansings. We don't do anything Christian. This does not create a problem with our clients. They know who we are before we come, or we don't come. We don't want to drive all the way to Orange County and have them find out who we are and then tell us that they don't want us in their house. We want them to know who we are and what we do before we come." Like most groups, ISIS does not use Ouija boards because they are doorways to another plane of existence. "If you are going to use a Ouija board, never use it alone," Dayna says, "because you would be very open to suggestion." The Orange County case that Dayna alluded to started with a Ouija board. "[The entity] ended up following [the clients] to their house. It all spiraled out of control from there. The daughter started getting bite marks on her arm that she couldn't explain," Dayna said. ISIS removed the troublesome entity by doing a cleansing. Pat and some of the other members who are Native American also did a "Rite of Crossing," a Native American ritual to help the spirit cross over.

Not surprisingly, some of the members of ISIS have been criticized for their pagan beliefs, but never on site: "We have run into some people who don't exactly practice what they preach, " Pat says. "Basically, some of us have been ridiculed in the street or via e-mail or in the store that I managed. A couple of Christians who came in told me that I was a 'devil worshipping, demon-loving witch' and that they were going to burn me at the stake. I looked them and the eye and said, 'You might try, but it won't be as easy this time. We won't walk meekly to the stake to be burned, and we might just take you with us.' And then I kicked them out of the store." Apparently, the persecution of witches in the twenty-first century will be much more difficult to pull off than it was in Salem three hundred years ago.

ISIS also differs from other New England groups in that its co-directors are not strong supporters of the *Ghost Hunters* televivision show on the Sci-Fi Channel. Dayna admits that TAPS has inspired a lot of people to form their own groups, but sometimes at the expense of cemeteries: "Our group respects cemeteries as historical monuments, but some monuments have been destroyed [by vandals posing as ghost hunters.] Some people have been trespassing into cemeteries. If we don't have permission, we don't go." Dayna also thinks that *Ghost Hunters* perpetuates a false impression of what paranormal investigators really do: "They don't show the long, tedious hours. They don't show all the work that goes on behind it. On *Ghost Hunters*, there is a lot of arguing going on and not enough working together. I think it's more about getting ratings than about teaching people how it's done."

Recently, the co-directors of ISIS have been trying to make peace with the paranormal community. "We are a unique group. We don't do things like the other groups do," Dayna says. "We use electronic equipment and our psychic abilities to get the best of both worlds, but a lot of Christian groups frown on what we do." Dayna says that the members of ISIS have bonded with Western Europe Paranormal and have attended some of the group's gatherings. Essentially, though, ISIS operates in its own sphere. "For the most part, we are pretty much out there on our own," Dayna says, "because if you say one thing wrong, you are pretty much blackballed by the paranormal community."

SIGNS
Chicopee, Massachusetts
Tammy Biller, Director
www.spiritsigns.org

Like many directors, Tammy Biller's desire to form her own group was sparked by curiosity regarding strange occurrences within her own home: "After staying there five years, I started questioning what was going on, and it just progressed from there," Tammy said. She founded her group, SIGNS: scientific investigations of ghosts n spirits, in 2004 with only five members, most of whom were friends of hers. Now her groups consists of a "hodgepodge" of investigators, including people who work in technology, a junior high school teacher, a cable repairman, a former cab driver, and an administrator in an electronics company.

Even though Tammy is the only sensitive in a group that employs the scientific approach, her group does not base its investigations around her abilities. "I help to guide the members to areas where there is energy present," Tammy said. "We use my psychic abilities just like we would use an EMF detector or thermometer. My job is to validate something that happens or that we uncover in our research."

SIGNS has investigated several historic sites on the Mohawk Trail, but the group is more interested in the disturbances that afflict ordinary people in their own homes. Tammy said, "Our mission is to help people in need, people who come up and say, 'I think I'm losing my mind.' Or they say, 'Every night at two o'clock in the morning the walls are shaking and the walls are banging. I don't know what's going on.'" Putting her clients' minds at ease is much more important to Tammy than collecting evidence of the paranormal. "We tell the homeowners in the very beginning that we are not going to make something up just so we can say we collected some evidence."

Although Tammy is not very impressed by the presence of orbs in the photographs taken by her group on investigations, she does not dismiss them out of hand: "We have a couple of orb pictures that we think might be something. You have to judge the situation. What was in the room? Was carpeting on the floor? Were there bugs? How solid is it? Is there movement? Is there a trail? What was the shutter speed? Was too much light in the picture? We ask a lot of questions when we look at pictures of orbs."

EVPs, on the other hand, are more significant, from Tammy's point of view, but they are not the best evidence. "I put a little more stock in EVPs, provided that they were recorded in a room where no one was present," Tammy said. "We can hear an EVP more clearly if we filter it out the noise on our computer." Photographs, Tammy believes, are much more convincing: "What I am really looking for is photographic evidence, like a mist or a full-body apparition." One of these sensational photographs was taken by one of her members, John, and it is featured on the group's web site. The group is so proud of the eerie photograph that members had it printed on their T-shirts.

SIGNS's most memorable investigation took place in a twenty-six-room mansion called The Victorian House. The Victorian House was abandoned for twenty years until it was purchased and renovated in 2000. Tammy believes that the extensive remodeling "stirred up" the spirits: "People have seen apparitions. They have had objects turn up missing and come back again. The new owner even saw a little boy down in the basement." The Victorian House's reputation is so widespread in New England that it has been investigated by a number of ghost-hunting groups, including TAPS. It has also been featured on the Travel Channel. SIGNS has conducted three investigations there, including one that will be featured in a television documentary.

Tammy will never forget the group's first visit to the old house: "The first time we were there, another member and I were sitting at the monitors—we had six monitors going. All of a sudden, she turned to me and said, 'My hair!' I looked at her, and her hair was standing straight up." Frantically, Tammy tried to find a camera while she was watching her friend. All the while, she counted in her head. By the time she got to "thirty," her friend's hair fell back down, just a few seconds before Tammy could locate her camera. "This was our weirdest moment there," Tammy said.

However, this incident was not the only weird encounter that Tammy had at The Victorian Mansion. "The next time we went back, we were walking on the third floor," Tammy said. "As we turned the corner, our EMF detector started going off. At the same time, we heard the sound of a man breathing right next to us." While experiences like this one are unsettling, even to veteran investigators, this case was extremely significant because the EMF detector verified the spectral breathing.

The Victorian House investigation shows that sometimes investigating takes a heavy toll on the investigators: "The girl whose hair stood up in The Victorian Mansion is no longer an active member," Tammy said. "After a couple of other scary experiences, she now just reviews evidence." Because fear is a normal response to bizarre occurrences, Tammy is not ashamed of her friend or any other member who feels compelled to run away when afraid. She does, however, encourage her group members to fight their fears, especially while investigating a private residence: "I tell them to calmly remove themselves from the situation." One way to reduce the "fear factor," Tammy believes, is to pair up people on investigations so that no one ever feels like he or she is totally alone. Working in teams of two or three also adds credibility to the investigators' personal experiences. "Members can back up each other's story if something happens," Tammy says. "Before each investigation, we decide who to put together and who not to put together." Compatibility, it seems, is a crucial element of any group effort, especially ghost hunting.

The success of SIGNS, Tammy believes, is proof that the Internet has been a boon to the field of paranormal investigating in the second millennium: "Shadowlands and some of the other big web sites are really helping [publicize the group]. The Internet also helps us to interact with other groups." Still, there is no substitute for one-on-one contact, especially when one is trying to get the word out and form bonds with other groups. "We're going to Gettysburg in June, and we'll meet with other groups while we are there. We have also made trips to Salem and Cape Cod." One of the most effective means of publicizing her group is the printed word. "I pass out business cards and magnets when I lecture at the university. We even have the URL of our web site on our cars. It is not at all unusual for people to stop us in a parking lot and ask us what we do." SIGNS, it appears, has found a way to make low technology and high technology work together, which is no easy task.

CAPE AND ISLANDS PARANORMAL RESEARCH SOCIETY
Manomet, Massachusetts
Derek Bartlett, Director
www.caiprs.com

Derek Bartlett, the founder and director of Cape and Islands Paranormal Research Society (CAIPRS), has modified his motivation for investigating the paranormal over the years: "If you had asked me the mission of my group three years ago, I would have said, 'Looking for the existence of ghosts.'" These days, Bartlett and his team members enjoy being the "last resort" for homeowners who are ill-equipped to deal with paranormal disturbances. "They know their house is haunted, or they wouldn't be calling us," Derek says. "We are there for people who call us up because they have nowhere else to turn."

Derek's mother is directly responsible for instilling in him an interest in the paranormal. "When I was a child, my Mom told me ghost stories instead of the Knights of the Round Table. As I was growing up, I watched the 'Kolchak' [i.e., *The Night Stalker*] series, *In Search Of*, and *That's Incredible*, and it progressed from there," Derek said. "When I was in the Marine Corps, I went to old forts, waiting to have the experience that never happened. After the Marine Corps, I kind of lost interest, but in the year 2000, I went to Hartford, Vermont, on my honeymoon, and I took some photographs of a masseuse sitting on the bed. When I got home, I developed the picture of the masseuse, and [her image] is very blurry. It looks like there is a figure standing behind her, but there are also streaks of light in the middle of the picture. It's like someone took a lightning bolt and threw it. It has a flicker of lights at both ends." Unsure of the validity of what he had photographed, Derek showed the photograph to a group in Massachusetts, and the next day, the picture appeared on the group's web site. "They are defunct, and [the picture] is on my web site now," Derek said.

This unnerving experience motivated Derek to do the research and to find out what it takes to be a real ghost hunter. "I read everything for months to find out what was the best way to investigate the paranormal. I've now gone from a one-man ghost-hunting team in 2000 to a nonprofit corporation today." Derek's group now has eighteen members. The composition of Derek's group reflects the broad appeal of ghost hunting. Derek is a business promoter for a software company. The membership of CAIPRS also includes a woman who keeps medical records, a prenatal care nurse, a telemarketer, a woman who owns her own business, a home adjuster for an insurance company, a homemaker, and a woman who works in the loan department. Derek gave one of the most important roles in any paranormal group—historical researcher—to a thirteen-year-old student with a love of history. Thrill seekers are not welcome in CAIPRS. "We tend not to allow adrenaline junkies in the group," Derek said. "We just want pragmatic people with open minds."

Keeping the group in the public eye is almost a full-time job in itself. "We send out newsletters to people who want to subscribe," Derek says. "We put up brochures through our local chamber of congress. We give free lectures at the college, and we always hand out business cards. We occasionally get television coverage when we do special investigations. We also do a lot of public service announcements for our local cable station."

CAIPRS is a science-based group whose members utilize any tools that help them get results. "We use our equipment to measure fluctuations in the environment," Derek says. The group's equipment includes ion particle counters, tri-field meters, video cameras, wireless video cameras, thermal temperature readers, remote temperature hydrometers, and even a hand-held mini-weather system. The sensitives on Derek's team are just another tool in his "tool box": "We will use sensitives to see if there is anything to record with our scientific equipment. Ninety-nine percent of the time, there isn't. This doesn't mean that there aren't any real sensitives. It just means that scientifically, I haven't been able to prove that there are." During a retrieval at an eighteenth-century home, Derek and some of his team members sat in on a séance and tried, unsuccessfully, to detect any paranormal activity with their equipment. He has had better luck using sensitives to supplement or substantiate previous information he has gained about the site. "We get the facts from the homeowners and the equipment, but the sensitives might stumble across additional information that they make note of during an investigation," Derek said.

Derek also employed the psychic abilities of one of his members during a soul retrieval. "The homeowners had asked me to find somebody who could stop the haunting," Derek said. "I only used her [the sensitive] once, but it did work." He has also called up the clergy to help stop a haunting, although, contrary to public belief, some homeowners do not want someone with a Christian background to expel a spirit from their house.

Unlike many investigators, Derek does not dismiss all orbs as unreliable evidence: "I have captured some anomalies that are orblike. For example, I once photographed an orb with a tail. On several investigations, our video cameras have captured solid balls flying around a corner and coming back fifteen or twenty feet. There are other orbs that are large when they get near you and small when they go away. These must be energy-based anomalies. That's all I can say." While he is not convinced that orbs are paranormal in origin, he says that he has never caught an orb with a video camera or still camera in a house that was not haunted.

Derek has a much lower opinion of EVPs. In 2004, his opinion of orbs changed when he began looking closely at the way most EVPs are recorded. "All of a sudden, I realized that you can create EVPs by rubbing the voice recorder against your jacket. I don't think it is a coincidence that the people who hold their recorders often get more EVPs than they would if the recorder was stationary." An even closer look at EVPs revealed that most of them are in English. "If I speak English and I hear an EVP, I'm going to put English to it. However, there is a lot of Old English still spoken in my home town of Plymouth, and I have yet to hear an Old English EVP. There are also a lot of Portuguese people around where I live, but I have never heard a Portuguese EVP either." The only EVPs that really challenge Derek's disbelief are those that are direct responses to questions asked by the investigator.

Five years after founding his group, Derek found out how dangerous ghost hunting can really be. "I was doing an investigation in Everett, Massachusetts," Derek said. "When I came back home, I was tired for a couple of days. Then my personality started changing. My interest in ghost hunting began to diminish. My behavior toward my team members became short and abrupt, like they were bothering me. I turned into this negative thing with destructive behavior." Before long, his team members noticed that Derek was drinking more heavily and that he was no longer an "upbeat" person. His eyebrows became pursed, and his cheeks were hollow. They began e-mailing questions to each other, like "What's going on with Derek?" "I didn't know this was happening," Derek said. "Life was a little complicated and a little stressful, but I was still me. And then I started having experiences at my house at the same time. For example, I saw a black cloud coming from my office. I heard things in the kitchen at night. I saw images in the living room." Derek credits a team member, Tom Durran, with helping him turn his life back around: "He came in at the request of my girlfriend and some of the team members to do a cleansing. He used the metaphysical style of cleansing—the sweetgrass and sage—and gave me some stones to hold on to. He theorized that it was something that was attacking me." Derek did not notice any immediate difference in himself after Tom cleansed the house, but after a while, his life took a turn for the better. His old personality returned, and his destructive behavior, especially his heavy drinking, vanished. Now, he is much more careful when he goes out on a case. "Is the thing entirely gone? Maybe, maybe not. Lately, I've been going into investigations really guarded."

Derek's healing by Tom Durran also resulted in the loss of an ability he had had since he was fourteen years old. "In eighth grade, I was a bad child," Tom said. "I was so bad that I was held back a year. In my second year of the eighth grade, I got a persistent cough. I couldn't shake it. That's when I found myself starting to hear voices. Down through the years, I continued to hear the voices of men, women, and children. They weren't complete sentences. They were parts of sentences—'Over here!' 'Over there!' 'Look there!' I am sure that this was not my subconscious talking to me. They were actual voices. I didn't hear them every day, just once or twice a week. These voices never said anything bad all the time that I was hearing them." However, the night Derek returned home from the Everett case, the tone of the voices became much more sinister: "I grabbed the door handle, and I heard, 'Kill all the animals!' It was the first negative thing I'd ever heard. Then the next day, I heard, 'Kill her!' After Tom cleansed the house, I lost the ability altogether." Derek is not really unhappy that the voices are gone, but he is glad that he began hearing them when he did: "In eighth grade when I began hearing the voices, my personality changed. I went through four years of high school without missing a single day of school. My anger was gone. I totally changed." Derek heard the voices from 1987 until 2005.

That one investigation that has "haunted" Derek all these years was conducted in Granville, Massachusetts, in a house built in the 1800s for a Civil War dignitary. "The woman who owned the house called us in because she was having problems. Her parents moved into it when she was a teenager, and she inherited the house years later." The homeowner told Derek that when she was young, she occasionally saw weird shapes in the windows as she walked down the hallway. Her encounters with the spirits continued when she moved back into the house in her thirties. "She started to drink due to the fact that she didn't want to see the ghosts and interact with them," Derek said.

On September 16, 2005, CAIPRS made the three-and-a-half-hour drive to Granville. Derek and another team member were in the bedroom recording EVPs while the other team members were walking through the rest of the house. "I was holding my tape recorder, and the other guy was writing down the questions I asked. Things went fine until I said, 'I'm thirty-three years old. How old are you?' In a split second, I felt two knuckles strike my right shoulder blade. Then it felt like it would if you took your own hand and put it on the back of your neck. It was forcing my head downward and choking me at the same time. The entity seemed to be about my height or taller." There was only a foot and a half of space between Derek and the wall, making it nearly impossible for someone to sneak behind him. After what seemed an eternity, Derek dropped the tape recorder on the bed, walked out into the hallway, and cried.

After Derek explained to the other team members what had happened to him, he was surprised to learn that an investigator stationed two rooms over recorded a nine-degree increase in the temperature of the room. In addition, the ion particle counter recorded a charge in the air of positive eighteen. "This researcher was very skeptical," Derek said. "She had a degree in geology from Yale University and a degree in business law from Harvard, but she could not explain the nine-degree increase in temperature in the room." Later on, the group brought in a psychic, who clarified some of the mysteries surrounding the house. "She was able to tell us the whole history of the house," Derek said, "which coincided with what we found. In the late 1800s and the early 1900s, the house was used as a home for the pastor. The psychic told us that the man was about my height. She even told us his name." The psychic also developed a plausible theory for Derek's attack. She said that a number of very dominating women lived in the house, and one of them resented Derek's presence. "We believe that one of these women felt threatened because I was an alpha male and attacked me," Derek said. "For me, this is evidence of the existence of the paranormal. I still can't explain the nine-degree increase in temperature." Derek adds that this is the only investigation he has ever been on where all of his team members were afraid, including him.

BERKSHIRE PARANORMAL
North Adams, Massachusetts
Josh Mantello, Director
www.berkshireparanormal.com

Josh Mantello differs from many ghost hunters in that his interest in the paranormal did not begin with a bizarre experience he had as a child. "I was never a firm believer in ghosts growing up," Josh said. "With my father being a member of the Masonic Lodge, I had always heard of its being haunted. When I joined the lodge, I heard the stories myself." After Josh became a midnight police officer, he heard stories about hotels and bed-and-breakfasts that had guests who were paranormal investigators. One day, he contacted the director of the New England Ghost Project, and went on an overnight visit at a Masonic lodge called the Houghton Mansion. That night, Josh became hooked: "I thought it was an adrenaline rush being in the presence of a ghost. It was great."

In 2003, Josh founded Berkshire Paranormal with his father, Nick, and his brother-in-law, Greg. The group's mission is focused on documenting the paranormal activity at the Houghton Mansion. "We are there at least once a month doing some form of research. We don't do many private residences," Josh said. "They are picking up slowly, though. We haven't got as many as we like." The group's small number of investigations cannot be blamed on poor public relations efforts. "We have a good working relationship with the local newspaper," Josh said, "so any events that we do, we take to the local newspaper. A couple of weekends ago, we did a fund-raiser for the Houghton House with TAPS, and that got a lot of publicity in the newspaper. We just completed an eleven-week exploratory class with the local middle school on ghost hunting, and that got publicized. The majority of our publicity, though, is Internet related."

Membership in the lodge is not a prerequisite for joining the group, but Josh admits that it might seem that way to the casual observer: "It seems like most of our new members eventually become members of the lodge, which is kind of funny. It's a recruiting tour for both." Psychics and sensitives are not refused admittance into the group, even though Josh claims that Berkshire Paranormal is science based: "We have used psychics in the past, but we don't weigh their evidence as much as we do the scientific evidence because we want our evidence to be approved. It's tough to get the scientific community to accept psychic evidence." Josh cites the group's desire for validity as the primary reason why it uses EMF detectors, voice recorders, video, temperature gauges, and still cameras.

Not only does Berkshire Paranormal investigate the Houghton House, but it tries to help preserve and maintain the house as well. "The TAPS event was a fund raiser," Josh says. "Seventy-five people paid one hundred and seventy-five dollars each for the privilege of investigating with Jason and Grant. They got most of the share of the money, and we got ten percent, and most of that went to the mansion. None of the money we raise though fund-raisers goes to us; it all goes to the Houghton Mansion."

Josh's burning desire to raise money for the Houghton Mansion is due in part to his personal connection to the lodge. "I am a past master of the lodge, and so is my father," Josh said. "Greg will be master of the lodge next year." Because they all have keys, they can enter the lodge any time they want.

Like many investigators with a background in law enforcement, Josh uses his skills acquired through years of police work on his investigation: "As a police officer, people lie to you, so I have a natural disbelief in people I don't know. I always assume I am being lied to, so if people tell me their place is haunted, I don't believe them right away. I'm tougher on evidence because I'm a policeman. I want to find out the truth for myself." Josh adds, though, that his skepticism does not extend to the existence of ghosts, which he is trying to prove through his investigations.

Berkshire Paranormal does not reject all orbs out of hand. Josh has developed a scale for rating orbs. "If it's transparent and has a cellular look to it, it's probably a dust orb," Josh says. "If an orb is emitting its own light, and we have corroborating evidence, we might accept it as evidence." One of the best orbs Josh's group has collected appeared during an all-night investigation of the Houghton Mansion. Several members of his group were sitting in a room when they heard a loud noise coming from another room down the hall. Two of the investigators walked down the hall and into the room. One of them exclaimed, "I heard the sound coming from over here!" and pointed to a corner of the room. At that same moment, the other investigator took his photograph. "He's pointing to an orb in the photograph," Josh says. "It's not transparent. It looks like it's emanating its own light instead of reflecting back an electronic flash." Even though some orbs, like this one, are impressive, Josh is not ready to accept them as indisputable proof of ghosts.

Other investigations of the Houghton Mansion have proven to be fruitful as well. "There's activity all over the entire building, except for the main dance hall, which was added on by the Masonic Lodge," Josh says. "I like to go there because I know I will find something every time. I'll go there at three A.M., and I'll hear voices." During the TAPS investigation of the Houghton Mansion, several people had personal experiences. "One girl said that her shoulders were being massaged," Josh said.

On another visit to the Houghton Mansion, Josh took a photograph of a half-body apparition during the day. "It's a picture of the third-floor window in what used to be the servants' quarters," Josh says. "You can see a figure standing in the window looking down at me. It has long, wispy hair, and it looks like it is wearing an overcoat or a smoking jacket." Josh is willing to accept this photograph as evidence because it was taken when the sun went behind a grove of trees: "When the sun is bright, it sometimes creates a pattern on the window."

The group's favorite location inside the Houghton Mansion is the basement. According to the legend, people who sit in the basement for a long time eventually see a young girl who is only three or four feet tall. "She comes in and peeks around the corner at you," Josh says. "She is kind of shy. If you walk toward her, she disappears." While investigating the basement, Josh's group has captured shadows and light anomalies on their video camera. Josh says that on one occasion, the investigators could actually see orbs with their own eyes in the basement: "Then one of the investigators took of picture of me with his flash, and it blinded me. I said, 'What did you do that for?' He said, 'Your face was glowing, man!'" Unfortunately, nothing came out on the photograph because the investigator was using an infrared camera at the time.

Berkshire Paranormal also collected some fascinating evidence at one of the first places they investigated outside of the Houghton Mansion: the Charlemont Inn in Charlemont, Massachusetts. At one point during the investigation, Josh and two other investigators were standing in a room. "There was a little bedside table with a lamp sitting on it," Josh said. "It was one of those old-fashioned lamps with a knob that clicks when you turn it on or off. While we were standing in this room with our equipment in our hands, we could hear the click of the knob turning, and the light shut off." Josh's initial response was to turn to the other members and ask them why they had turned off the light; he stopped in mid-sentence when he noticed that their hands were full and they were about five feet away from the table. "This is the first time that I felt something was in the room with us," Josh said.

Josh had another encounter with an entity when in May 2006 he and another member of the group, Greg, stopped at a cemetery on the Mohawk Trail—Route 2 through Massachusetts—on their way back from a conference: "Greg opened the door and began climbing out of the car while he was taking pictures. I was looking behind the back seat for my digital voice recorder so I could collect some EVPs. As I stepped out of the car, Greg yelled, 'Get in the car! Get in the car! Run!' I wondered if he had seen a bear or a mountain lion or maybe somebody coming at him with a shotgun, but I didn't question him. We got in the car and drove away." On the way home, Greg said that he had seen a glowing figure weaving in and out of the headstones, coming at him at a running pace. "You know when someone runs, he bobs?" Gregg said. "This thing didn't bob. It came straight at me." Greg suspects that walking into the graveyard under a full moon might have stimulated some of the spirits. Not long thereafter, Josh and Greg returned to the graveyard, but the evidence they collected was a letdown after their previous visit. "We heard some weird noises in the woods and captured some good EVPs, but we did not see any apparitions," Josh said.

Josh is fully aware that if his caseload of private residences is ever to increase, he and his members must be careful not to offend anyone, especially the religious community: "We take an unbiased look at religion. If our client is Catholic, we offer up a good Catholic prayer. If the client is pagan, we offer up a pagan prayer. We try to keep religion out of our investigations the best we can."

DRAGONSTAR PARANORMAL & HEALING
Framington, Massachusetts
Jim Correia, Director
www.dragonstarparanormal.com

Jim Correia thanks television for getting him interested in the paranormal: "I have always been interested in things that couldn't be easily explained away. I began reading books about Bigfoot and the Loch Ness Monster as a boy. When *Sightings* and *Unsolved Mysteries* came on the air, I was hooked on ghosts. There's just something about psychic Peter James [on *Sightings*]. That look that he gets in his eyes when he's made contact with a ghost really freaked me out. [My interest] just increased from there and became an obsession. I think I read every book on ghosts in the library during junior high school." Not surprisingly, Jim founded his own group when he was seventeen years old.

DragonStar Paranormal & Healing came into being in August 2006. The group now has seventeen members, all of whom come from different backgrounds. "I have two gentlemen with a degree in television production, a photographer, and an EMT," Jim says. "I also have a nurse/massage therapist and another woman who is teacher of spirituality and a psychic." Jim works in retail sales, but he is a healer as well. He says he intentionally recruited people from an assortment of professions so that each person would bring something different to the group.

The mission of DragonStar Paranormal & Healing is neither to prove or disprove the paranormal. "We try to help our client to the fullest extent," Jim says. "If we disprove a haunting, we want to help our client figure out what is going on." Jim believes that fear of the paranormal is so strong in New England that a lot of people would rather fool themselves into believing that the disturbances in their home are being caused by knocking pipes instead of by something from the spirit world. Jim blames this stigma of the paranormal with making it difficult for him to find clients. "We have the hardest time getting some of the really good cases because they don't want people to know what's going on," Jim says. "I do a lot of client work, and people up here really want to be discrete. Even in Salem where the witch trials were held, we have trouble getting cases because people don't want to talk about it anymore." In fact, DragonStar Paranormal & Healing has encountered more resistance from governing boards, building owners, and homeowners than it has from the religious community.

On the other hand, New England is a mecca for paranormal investigators because of the large number of old insane asylums that are being renovated into condominiums. "If we're going to catch something, we'll catch it there," Jim says. A friend of Jim's is a professional photographer who has investigated the Tawnee Asylum and the Fox Asylum, and he is convinced that most of the activity in these old hospitals is residual in nature.

Of all the evidence that is collected by means of the group's EMF meters, temperature gauges, and a complete array of digital cameras, thirty-five-mm cameras, and video cameras, Jim is particularly impressed by orbs and EVPs. Jim pays close attention to orbs because, as he puts it, "It really takes a lot of energy for orbs to manifest. When you're in a room with no ventilation and you're seeing orbs the size of softballs or basketballs, there's got to be something there. You just can't say that all orbs are dust or pollen." Jim has taken so many photographs of orbs that he believes he can distinguish between genuine orbs and those that are insects or moisture. EVPs are even more amazing, from Jim's point of view. "Everything leaves an electronic impression," Jim says, "and if you're running a tape recorder or a camera, and something sticks on that, I really think something's there." One of the group's most startling EVPs was a voice saying somebody's name. "We caught the same EVP on a digital video camera and a voice recorder. This says a lot," Jim says.

Jim has never photographed a full-body apparition, but he has captured mists on film. "I was photographing a grassy lawn on a clear night when a mist suddenly appeared." He does not subscribe to the theory that strange mists or vapors are ectoplasm. "To be ectoplasm, [the mist or vapor] would have to be in an environment where it could not be smoke," Jim says. One of the most intriguing mists Jim has photographed was in a place where one would expect to find smoke: a bar. "When we were in Texas, we went to a bar, and as soon as I walked in, I could feel the presence of a spirit," Jim said. "A girl in the bar photographed a mist. She took another photograph, and the mist was there. They took a third picture, and it was gone." In an attempt to debunk the mist, Jim took two photographs of her inhaling and blowing out cigarette smoke. When they examined the photographs, they discovered that the consistency of the cigarette smoke was not nearly as thick as the mist in the photographs that had been taken earlier.

Jim's personal favorite of all his investigations was actually conducted in an old building by another team. Because the area was so large, the team broke up into two groups. One group went upstairs; Jim's group went downstairs. One of Jim's teammates was attacked while they were down there. "We had left the woman in the basement, and as we walked in, we could see something to the right standing there. It had glowing, orange eyes, and it just charged at her. She was running around me, trying to keep her back towards me. It was running behind her. I saw it. I was the first one to see the eyes." Jim regrets that the team disbanded before the evidence could be examined.

To prevent another occurrence like this one, Jim now has a demonologist/trained exorcist on his team. Because most people do not want to admit that they are living with an evil presence, they usually contact DragonStar Paranormal & Healing through a friend. So far, Jim has had six encounters with demons on investigations. Ironically, not all of his clients are upset when told that something evil is in their house. "One couple was relieved when we told them there was a demon in their house," Jason said. "They thought they were going crazy." After the group clears the house out and the client feels comfortable, the members leave.

Jim was involved in another intense situation in a cemetery in Texas while he was returning from a conference in Jefferson. "They've got a lot of unmarked graves," Jim says. "Several of the graves say 'Cherokee' on them." Jim was with his sister team at the time, and while they were walking around, they got the feeling that they were being watched. One of the women on the team said that something had hit her. She became so unnerved that they had to take her back to the car. "When we went back to the cemetery, there was a giant ball of light, right where the woman said she thought she got hit," Jim said. He also noticed that the area was very cold: "If you have ever been to Texas, you know that when it's hot, it's hot! That place was really cold. I remember this because there was a thunderstorm moving in, and when that happens, it starts to heat up a little. It was so cold that I had to put on a sweatshirt. A woman who has been there before says that in August, there is a twenty-degree difference in the cemetery." Jim's sister team has promised to take him back out to the cemetery the next time he returns to Texas.

Jim was satisfied with the working relationship he had with the other groups in New England until he visited with some of the paranormal research groups at the conference in Texas. "Down in Texas, they [the groups] get together and have a good time. My team has never gotten together with any other group in New England. The team I was with before didn't socialize with any other group either. People up here, though, don't want to share or work with each other. There's no camaraderie among the different groups in New England." Jim is so disillusioned with his situation in New England that he has vowed to move to Texas in the next few years.

Jim believes that the *Ghost Hunters* television show will recruit a new generation of paranormal investigators in the 2000s, much in the same way that *Sightings* and *Unsolved Mysteries* turned him into a ghost enthusiast back in the 1990s. Not only has *Ghost Hunters* made investigating trendy, but it has also removed the stigma that has attached itself to the field over the years: "If it weren't for TAPS, I don't think the paranormal community would be as accepted in society. I give those guys a lot of credit. They have basically opened a lot of doors for the rest of us. Now we can walk into a place and introduce ourselves as paranormal investigators, and people won't look at us like we have two heads."

THE NEW ENGLAND GHOST PROJECT
Dracut, Massachusetts
Ron Kolek and Maureen Wood, Co-Directors
www.neghostproject.com

Ron Kolek did not grow up believing in the paranormal. In fact, one could say that he became involved in the field of the paranormal by accident, literally: "I owned a woodworking manufacturing company years ago. After being in business for twenty-five years, I closed my woodworking factory because I couldn't compete overseas and started making kitchen cabinets. One day, I was working by myself, and I ran my hand through a table saw and cut my fingers off. They took me to the emergency room at three P.M." Thinking there was nothing they could do for Ron, the attendants kept him overnight in the emergency room until a specialist arrived and performed a six-and-a-half-hour operation. His fingers were reattached, but a cat scan revealed a pulmonary embolism. "I was transferred to the ICU, and while I was there, I experienced things that I don't understand to this day. I don't even like to talk about it much," Ron said. After Ron was released from the hospital, he could no longer do woodworking, so he enrolled in a course in television production. "I decided to do my class project on ghosts because of what had happened to my in the hospital. That's how it all got started," Ron said.

When Ron started his group, his wife thought he was crazy. She changed her mind, however, after his first investigation. "The first investigation I did was a very nice place. The woman opened her house to us and explained what was going on. From then on, my wife realized that people want us to come in and help them."

Ron did not believe in psychics until he met Maurreen Wood, who, unlike Ron, has had a lifelong fascination with the paranormal. "My mother never told me until years later that her mother had 'the gift,'" Maureen said. "When I was three years old, I had a near-death experience. I had meningitis, and I remember leaving my body and seeing my parents crying. I saw myself face down on the table with a tube sticking out of my spine." When Maureen was ten years old, she began having nightmares about people being murdered. She also started seeing apparitions in her bedroom. "To me, it was normal. My poor father thought there was something wrong with me. But my mother, who had had these experiences herself, said, 'You're normal. Not a problem.'" A few months later, she had an experience that changed her life. She was riding in the family car with her mother and several other children. Her mother parked the car so that she could pay some bills. "All of a sudden, I couldn't see anybody anymore," Maureen said. "Everything went black. It was like nighttime. Then I saw this mill in front of me, and it was burning." Maureen snapped out of it when her mother returned and slammed the car door shut. Two days later, the local mill burned to the ground. After Maureen told her mother about her vision, she arranged for Maureen to meet with a friend of hers who showed the girl how to control her psychic abilities. "When I grew up, I became a medium," Maureen said. "I performed séances for about three years."

Even though Maureen has been involved with the world of the paranormal much longer than Ron has, she also took an indirect route to becoming a paranormal investigator. One day in 2001, she told her husband, on a whim, that she would like to drive out to a little store that she had not visited in a long time. The proprietor recognized Maureen instantly. He walked over to her and said, "Maureen, I want you to have this." In his hand was a folded newspaper. "When I got home, I read the back of it, and Ron's monthly column for the New England Ghost Project was in there. I thought to myself, 'What the heck!' and I sent him an e-mail, explaining what I do. At this time, I didn't know if this stranger was going to kidnap me and take me to a desert island or not. My husband said that if this is what I wanted to do, I should do it. And that's how I joined the New England Ghost Project."

Diversity, Ron believes, is the key to the group's success. Aside from being a radio personality, he sells luggage. Maureen works as a technical instructor for a medical company. Ron believes that bringing a single point of view to an investigation not only is boring, but can taint the evidence as well. The only real prerequisite that the group has for membership is a level head. "We once had a girl [on our team] who was so into it that everything that happened was paranormal," Maureen said. "We'd turn the lights down, and she'd jump. It's easy to lose yourself when you experience the paranormal. You need to have that sense of balance on an investigation. It's almost like having one foot in this world and another foot in the other."

According to Ron, the mission of the New England Ghost Project is twofold: to inform and to investigate. For Ron personally, his primary objective is to prove the existence of the paranormal to himself. Maureen, however, believes that her job is to ease the fears of people by telling them what is really going on in their home or place of business: "A lot of times, helping is also verification for some people. They call us up and say, 'I think I'm going crazy. Could you please come and tell me if there's something in my house?' What is the point of doing what I do if I can't help people? That is the big thing for me." Maureen believes that part of her job is helping earthbound spirits cross over as well. She admits, though, that not all of the spirits they have encountered want to leave this plane of existence: "Many of the spirits we encounter don't want to move on. I'd say that thirty-five percent of them are really comfortable being right where they are."

Unlike some New England paranormal research teams, the New England Ghost Project does not visit a site with the intention of debunking the reported haunting. "We try to have an open mind," Ron says. "We're not there to prove or disprove. We gather evidence. Then we go through it and decide whether or not the place is haunted." Maureen admits, though, that not finding any evidence of paranormal activity is not proof that a place not haunted: "We've had a few investigations where we told the home-owner, 'We don't feel anything here, but we can't say for sure that your home is not haunted, because maybe there is something here when we are not around.'"

The New England Ghost Project is unique among New England groups because it has its own radio show on iTunes called *Ghost Hunters Spotlight*. Ron says, "We interview authors and scientists and show different points of view. Sometimes, people call us up on our radio show and tell us about their hauntings." A side benefit of the group's iTunes show is the bonds that have been created between the New England Ghost Project and other paranormal research groups in New England. "We did an investigation of North Adams with Berkshire Paranormal a while ago. Last Sunday we went out with members of three other groups on an investigation. We don't really have a connection with TAPS, though."

When the group is on a case, each person has a designated role. Ron speaks with the homeowners or the owner of the restaurant. Another member, Vaughn, maps out the place with the EMF meter to make sure that the group does not get any false readings from hidden wiring or electric appliances. Maureen walks around the building by herself and tries to communicate with the spirits in the place. She prefers not to know anything about the site, to enhance the validity of any information she gives the group. "There are times when I don't even know where we're going," Maureen says. "Ron will simply say, 'We're going on an investigation in New Hampshire two hours away.' He doesn't really give me the name of a place. I prefer it this way. I want to be 'clean' before I go out on an investigation." Unlike many directors who refuse to use psychics at all, Ron views Maureen as just another tool in his toolbox, like an EMF meter or a digital recorder: "The majority of the time, when Maureen makes contact, I pick up abnormal EMF readings. If we use Maureen alone, it's just her. But if we can bring in some additional evidence, it adds credibility to what she does."

Ron even goes so far as to say that Maureen adds a whole new dimension to his group: "Spirits are actually physically in her body. As a result, we've had a lot of physical altercations." In Haverhill, Massachusetts, a spirit that calls itself General Beauregard has expressed its hatred for Ron through Jane. Maureen believes she knows why the general dislikes Ron: "Sometimes when I channel spirits, Ron can tell when I am being adversely affected, and he'll try to stop the communication. I think that sometimes the spirits are irritated with him."

On one investigation, Maureen was actually accosted by one of the spirits she was channeling. "Sometimes when we are conducting an investigation we encounter something that's not so nice," Maureen says. "Sometimes it has a negative attitude. On one investigation, I heard a voice screaming, 'Get out!' It turned out that one of our investigators picked up the same voice on an EVP." When Maureen told Ron that they were not welcome in the house, he exclaimed, "No, we're not leaving! I'm not afraid! If you have anything else to say, say it!" At that moment, Maureen doubled over in pain. "It was like I was sucker punched," Maureen said.

Maureen had another physical encounter during an investigation of the 1859 House. "[The spirit] was very angry at being murdered," Maureen said. "I got my EMF meter, and while I was taking readings, something was glowing over our heads. I then had the sensations of a spirit entering my body. The next thing I know, I'm down for the count on the floor." Maureen does not recall intentionally antagonizing the spirit, but now she is much more careful about what she says and thinks in the presence of a ghost.

Ron believes that spirits like the general or the one who attacked Maureen do not deserve respect. "They are probably the same way now as they were when they were alive," Ron says. Maureen, on the other hand, is much more understanding: "How do you feel when you're having a really bad day? You can't get over it. When you finally get the chance to vent to somebody, you feel better because you let it all out and you are finally able to move on. If the spirits I meet are angry and they need to get the last word out, then maybe letting them channel through me allows them to vent a little bit." Unlike some investigators who deliberately antagonize spirits in order to get them to manifest themselves somehow, Maureen simply tells them, "If you've got something to say, then say it. Don't play games!"

Because Ron is so concerned about Maureen's well-being and the well-being of the other members as well, he encourages them to carry protection along with them on investigations. "I'm a devout Catholic," Ron says. "I've studied exorcism in the Catholic Church. I've even accompanied an exorcist before, so I am big on protection. We say St. Michael's prayer before every investigation. I also pass out vials of holy water to everyone who wants it." On one investigation, one of the newer members chose not to carry holy water with her. Interestingly enough, she was the only member of the group who became violently ill. Holy water came in handy once again when Ron was working on a television segment at an old cemetery. "We had six batteries with us for our camcorder. They should have lasted hours," Ron says. "But between all of them, they lasted only fifteen minutes. The next time we went out there, I brought holy water with me, and we had no problems." Maureen is also convinced of the power of the holy water, but she also believes that its ability to protect the user depends on the intent behind it.

Sometimes Ron brings along to investigations a concoction of holy water and other ingredients that he calls his "special mix." His "mix" was in his pocket one day when the group visited New England's Stonehenge, a group of stone megaliths located in southern New Hampshire. Because the group was investigating in late afternoon, no one really expected to collect any significant evidence. "We started getting some readings while we were there," Ron said, "and I could sense that an Indian was trying to get through [to me]. "I said to the entity, 'Not now! Not now!'" A few minutes later, Maureen and Ron climbed into their car and drove off. All of a sudden, Maureen started feeling the energy surge again. At the same moment, Ron's EMF meter started going off. His first thought was that they had driven under some high-tension wires. When he realized that there were no high-tension wires in the vicinity, he reached in his pocket for his "special mix." Before he had a chance to spray it inside the car, the entity was gone. Ron stopped the car, turned to Maureen, and said, "Can you drive?" Maureen replied, "I don't know. Let's find out." A few minutes later, they stopped at a Wendy's (restaurant) and checked out their

EMF meter. "The funny thing was that the EMF meter wasn't even on," Maureen said. "It was turned off when it started going off inside the car. Ron checked the batteries, and they had welded themselves to the inside of the meter."

Occasionally, the group is called in to cleanse a house. Sometimes, they bring along specialists. "I have a group of friends who do that," Maureen says. "They do cleansings of homes. They try to find out who these spirits are and what they want. I've done blessings before, but I like to have people with me who know what they're doing." The group consulted one of these specialists during an investigation of a nineteenth-century home. The young couple who had moved in built a second story on top of the house. While they were renovating the house, they found some human bones behind a wall. They also learned that a man had committed suicide in the house. They had not lived in the house very long before strange things started happening. Tentacles of smoke curled out of the closet. Toys began moving by themselves. Occasionally, the couple detected cold spots in the house. After the husband was thrown violently out of bed, the couple decided to contact Ron Kolek. On the initial walk-through, he noticed a shadow in a closet leading to the baby's room. Ron returned a few days later with several other members, including a sensitive named Brian. Brian had not been in the house for very long before he revealed the source of the activity to Ron: "It's got nothing to do with the land or the bones in the wall. Whatever is here is not human. It wants the baby." Ron was not surprised when the husband told him that the child had not been baptized, even though they were Catholic. "I suggested that they baptize the boy, and they agreed," Ron said. "After that, all of the trouble in the house stopped. I still see that boy in church, and they've never had to call me back."

Ron has been in situations where the spirits have actually "reached out and touched" people. One evening, Ron went out to Old Hill Cemetery in New Freeport, accompanied by two other members, Brian and Mark. "I was shooting one of the graves, and my entire forearm, from the wrist to the elbow, became covered with a black, thick, oozy gunk." During an investigation of the Tortilla Flats restaurant in New Hampshire, which had been a stop on the Underground Railroad, Ron interviewed a waitress who had had the same dark, gelatinous substance creep up her arm. "I know of four other cases where this has happened," Ron says. "I can't say it was ectoplasm, though, because we don't really know what ectoplasm is."

Maureen's most memorable investigation took place at a lighthouse that was reportedly haunted by the ghost of the wife of the last lighthouse keeper. "We were doing the investigation in a really small room," Maureen says. "There was a little hallway, and we lined up at the end of the hall. I started channeling, and I was getting her name—Carney—and I learned that she died of old age and that she was at peace. Then I heard a voice telling me, 'Push her out! Push her out!' The next thing I know, I'm looking down at myself lying on the floor, and I see Ron trying to lift me up and put me in a chair. Finally, I returned to my body. Ron looked like he had seen a ghost." After regaining her composure, Maureen walked downstairs and began talking to a woman who was a local storyteller. Suddenly, Maureen recalled something that Carney had told her while she was in her trance: "Thank you very much for the pink flowers." She mentioned this statement to the storyteller and was surprised to learn that her husband had surreptitiously placed pink tulips—Carney's favorite flowers—in her coffin and closed the lid. When the storyteller showed Maureen a picture of Carney, she broke down completely. "I couldn't stop crying because I could feel her energy again," Maureen said. "Usually, when I'm channeling somebody, I don't see them, but I sure did this time."

Maureen had another memorable encounter at the Hoover Mansion in North Adams, Massachusetts. According to the local legend, Hoover's daughter, Mary, fell in love with her chauffeur, John Willard, but her father disapproved. After Mary died, Willard committed suicide. Maureen became personally involved in the family dispute while she was touring the house. "The other people were walking around downstairs," Maureen said. "I went upstairs and sat in Mary's chair. Suddenly, I started channeling Mary. Then the next thing I know, Mr. Hoover came through, and he was angry. He was swearing. Then he tried to drag me out of the chair." At this point, Maureen lost consciousness for about ten minutes. When she recovered, she was in a lot of pain. "It was like I was having a heart attack," Maureen said. "It was a week before I could build my energy back up." This was a particularly unusual experience for her because as a rule, when she channels a spirits, she is unable to recall what had happened.

The Windham Restaurant in Windham, New Hampshire, also provided the New England Ghost Project with some unforgettable moments. On one visit, one of the members photographed the image of the face of a little boy. "We took another photograph at the same spot just a few seconds later, and the face was gone," Maureen said. "It was replaced by a streak of light going straight up into the ceiling." During another investigation at the Windham Restaurant, the group was being interviewed by a reporter. During the interview, Maureen had the feeling that the reporter, Brian Bates, thought she was crazy. Then something happened that confirmed Maureen's stories about the place. "The next thing I know, the coffee pot behind me turns on and starts pouring coffee," Maureen says. "Everyone jumps a mile high. At the same time, the temperature gauge dropped to 66.6 degrees. Brian Bates comes over and—honest to God—he's white as a ghost. He was so terrified." By the time the reporter had left the Windham Restaurant, he had changed his mind about people who have experienced paranormal events.

Not all of the group's investigations have been terrifying. During an investigation of a haunted strip club, Ron encountered an orb that he is fairly certain was not flecks of dust. "This stripper was dancing, and an orb was spinning around a pole next to her." Maureen says that the group did not get a clear view of the orb because "for some reason, the camera was focused on the stripper the whole time." It goes without saying that the person filming the orb was one of the male members of the group.

Ron and Maureen credit the current surge of interest in the paranormal to popular television shows like *Ghost Hunters*, *A Haunting*, *Supernatural*, and *Ghost Whisperer*. They admit that even though more people believe in the paranormal than ever before, a large number of people are not receptive to the possibility that ghosts might exist. "Some disbelievers are thinking in terms of computers," Maureen says. "If something doesn't compute, they are not going to accept it. To try to get people to believe in something that is outside of their comfort zone is illogical."

NEW HAMPSHIRE

NEW HAMPSHIRE PARANORMAL
Manchester, New Hampshire
Liz Howard and Tara McNeely, Co-Directors
newhampshireparanormal.com

Liz Howard comes by her interest in the spirit world naturally. "I am a preacher's daughter. Even though my father was very strict [in his insistence that ghosts do not exist], I grew up believing that there was something out there other than what he taught me. He thinks I'm crazy because I hunt ghosts. He always asks me if I've found Elvis yet." Ironically, Liz's mother is a member of New Hampshire Paranormal.

Liz started her group in 2006 with three people. Aside from being a stay-at-home mom, Liz also works as a freelance photographer and a graphic designer, part-time. Her members also have a variety of outside jobs. "One of my members works at PETCO," Liz says. "My Mom works at a store. We have a couple of students. One of our guys delivered pizza, and another worked for a security agency." What her diverse group has in common is their tendency to be very analytical during an investigation. "We're not going to hear a noise and say, 'Oh, there's a ghost.' We always try to debunk a haunting," Liz says.

New Hampshire Paranormal promotes itself primarily through the Internet and word of mouth. Liz had a number of T-shirts made with the group's name emblazoned on the front, but her members were not pleased with the result. "I'm the only one who has a T-shirt," Liz says. "I would like to have more made, but the cheapest places want us to buy one hundred T-shirts."

She says that the mission of her group is "to prove that we are not alone. It is a passion of ours." Even though Liz describes her group's approach to investigations as science based, she admits that they use dowsing rods. On one of her investigations, Tara McNeely's dowsing rods provided one of the evening's most frightening moments. "On the end of each dowsing rod is a little bulb that is screwed on," Tara said. "I was in the woods with one of our other members. We were walking along when we heard something hit the ground. We started looking among the leaves and discovered that it was one of our dowsing rods. I screwed the ends really tight on both rods. By the time we left the woods, both balls had fallen off again. This had never happened before."

As far as the evidence collected through electronic equipment is concerned, Liz is not impressed by orbs, but EVPs are another matter entirely. "We've recorded some really good ones," Liz said. "All of our EVPs are in English. Now that I think about it, if we captured [a voice] that wasn't in English, we probably wouldn't know it."

The investigations that have made the biggest impression on Liz and Tara are their visits to a wooded area in Pembroke, New Hampshire. Tara first discovered this place while doing research for a book. "In 1875, a girl was murdered in Pembroke," Tara said. "She was on her way to school at nine A.M. when she was killed. There is a monument to here where she was murdered and decapitated. They have stone markers, one where her head was found, and one where her body was found. I have spent a lot of time in the woods, and I've noticed that sometimes the wind would blow and the trees wouldn't move. Or the trees would move when the wind wasn't blowing." Tara wishes that the spot were more secluded than it actually is: "It's become a hang-out for teenagers on the weekend. They leave beer bottles all over the place and make a big mess."

One night, Tara was walking through the woods with a few friends, searching for the murder site. They had been out in the woods for six hours when they decided it was time to go home. "We walked down the road, and there was something hazy by the monument," Tara said, "not a full-bodied apparition, just a haze. We agreed that it was probably the ghost of the murdered girl."

On another nightly trek through the woods, Liz and Tara decided to investigate the wooded site by themselves. They hadn't been at the murder site very long when Liz became terrified. "I was pretty close to losing it myself," Liz said. The women set up their camera near the monument closest to the road. "Liz was walking around taking pictures, and I decided that I was going to sit on the monument and do some EVP work," Tara said. "We were there for less than half an hour." Liz believed that because she knew the name of the dead girl, she might have a better chance of recording some EVPs. She was asking questions like "What's your favorite food?" and "What's your favorite color?" when she noticed that it was getting colder, so cold that her left leg felt like it was frozen. Liz decided to play back the tape to see if she had gotten any EVPs, but no voices were recorded other than her own. The women then reviewed their camcorder, which they use as a fail-safe. "The tape was about to end just before we were getting ready to leave," Liz said. " I called her name for the last time. Then a couple of seconds later, we heard a whisper, and it said, 'Hello.' We only heard it on the tape when we played it back." Liz hastened to point out the woods were very quiet that evening because traffic on the road was very slow.

On Tara's next visit to the site, she was accompanied with four other members. Liz was not with them. "We were all circled around the body marker, which is a two- to three-foot post. I looked around me and noticed for the first time that the five dead trees surrounding the body marker formed the shape of a heart. I'd never noticed that before." Tara's job that night was to collect EVPs. She called the dead girl's name in an effort to lure her out of hiding. After a few minutes Tara noticed that the wind was blowing, but the trees were not moving. After first, she thought that she and the others did not see the trees move because it was so dark and because the tops of the trees were so high off the ground. Then she began to listen more closely to the sound of the wind. "It started sounding less and less like wind and more like some-one brushing against the underbrush," Tara said. "At first, it was kind of faint. Then the sound became more focused in one spot, and it wasn't above us anymore. Then it started sounding more like footsteps over the leaves on a lighted path. We think the noise we heard was the sound of the dead girl's feet and dress hitting the underbrush as she walked along. Eventually, the walking sound stopped about fifty feet from me." Tara and the other four investi-gators are certain that no animals were passing through the woods that night, because a nearby streetlight illuminated the spot where they were standing, and they saw no cats, dogs, or smaller animals in the area. Unfortunately, neither their tape recorders nor their voice recorders picked up the eerie noise.

Another place where New Hampshire Paranormal has had some very strange experiences is Gibson Cemetery. Liz says that this old cemetery is her favorite place to go ghost hunting: "We've caught more things there than anywhere else. "We have gotten a lot of EVPs. I've been touched by an unseen presence out there. I've also seen a shadow out there. Several of us have heard drums beating in the background, kind of like tribal drums." Liz believes that the drum sounds the group has heard in Gibson Cemetery were residual sounds made by the spirits of the Native Americans who lived in the area years before.

Liz is grateful that New Hampshire Paranormal has received no negative feedback from any religious people so far. Tara credits the group's peaceful coexistence with the Christian community to the fact that so many Catholics live in New Hampshire and Rhode Island. "Catholics are very open to the possibility of spirits," Tara said. "If we lived a little further north, [what we do] would seem a little weird to some people."

GRANITE STATE PARANORMAL
Washington, New Hampshire
Jim Snell, Director
granitestateparanormal.50megs.com

Jim Snell credits growing up in New England with infecting him with "ghost fever." "As a kid, I was really interested in ghost stories, and growing up in New England, I [soon discovered] that there were plenty of them around." He founded Granite State Paranormal in 2005. The group now has approximately thirty members, all of whom place more faith in scientific equipment than in psychics. "We don't use psychics," Jim says. "One time, we worked on a television show with several psychics. To be honest, I wasn't very impressed." In Granite State Paranormal's investigations, science and history combine, Jim believes, to help make the field of paranormal investigating more respectable: "Several members of my group are deeply interested in history. I've always been a history buff as well. [I am really happy to see] that history and science are beginning to merge [in ghost hunting]." Jim singles out tape recorders and infrared cameras as the types of equipment that are taking paranormal investigating to the next level.

Like TAPS, Granite State Paranormal sets out trying to debunk hauntings using scientific equipment. Jim has found EMF detectors to be particularly useful in debunking hauntings. He believes that extreme EMF fields have the capacity to cause people to hallucinate: "We had a case where a woman woke up in bed and saw a manifestation, so she called us in. We checked it out, and it turned out to be an 'off-the-wall' bubble of EMF." The homeowners had a small partition wall under the bed, and the space was filled with wiring for the refrigerator and the microwave oven. Sometimes these electrical fields interfere. "We explore all possibilities, and we suggest that the landlords take care of these electronic fields. For us, the EMF detector is not really a ghost detector, like it is portrayed on television."

The interest in paranormal investigations that has been generated by TAPS has a down side, according to Jim: "All of a sudden, we get all of these phone calls. Everybody thinks every little hair ball they catch on film is a ghost." In one case, a homeowner told Jim said that he heard a ghost walking down the hall behind him: "I sent one of my people down under the house and found that he had three- to four-inch PVC sewer pipe held up between the joists with a piece of duct tape. So every time he flushed the toilet or got a drink of water or walked down the hall, it swung and knocked between the joists." When confronted with the evidence, a number of homeowners do not take the news very well: "You can take them by the hand and show them [the cause of the disturbance], and they still want to believe that a ghost caused the noise. In this case, the man was offended because we disproved the haunting."

Because dealing with the public can be problematic, Jim prefers to investigate historic sites: "Dealing with the historical places, like the grand hotels, is much more productive because you are not dealing with drug use or mental illness. At a grand hotel, you've got a hundred employees, and maybe ten of them have had an experience, so that broadens the spectrum of believability."

Jim believes that keeping the group in the public eye has a definite impact on the number of requests they receive for investigations every year. "We had a radio show," Jim says. "We also get a lot of attention during Halloween. We give lectures, too. Not long ago, Borders called us up and wanted us to do an investigation there. It's been a tremendous venue for us, and I think that's where most people have heard of us." Granite State Paranormal's reputation as being the largest paranormal investigating group in New Hampshire has had its perks as well. "When we did the Mt. Washington Hotel, they probably spent $3,500 in comps. They gave us suites and room service," Jim says. Being famous has also gained the group admittance in places that have been closed to investigators for years. "The first time we did a lighthouse, it was closed by the Coast Guard. The place is locked up now, but they allowed us to check the place out all night long. When people hear that we investigated there, it impresses other venues, and that opens even more doors for us."

Jim does not care much for photographic evidence, especially pictures of orbs, which are usually nothing more than dust or moisture. "If you see [an orb] with the naked eye, though, that's different," Jim says. EVPS are much more interesting, from Jim's point of view: "EVPs are very easy to get. We have gotten EVPs on two-thirds of our cases." Jim places so much weight on sound evidence partially because he is an independent radio and television producer. "I also do scoring for films," Jim says. "I've been in broadcasting for quite some time. I used to be a radio DJ. I have also done some films for the Catholic Church. When you are independent, you do whatever comes around."

So far, none of the members of the members of Granite State Paranormal have been frightened on an investigation. "I've got to hand it to my team," Jim says. "We've been to some pretty sketchy places. They're so into the science and making sure the equipment is set up. You're so busy that [a site] becomes a work environment." He admits, though, that the group's training sessions tend to "weed out" the more timid members: "Our case manager does a good job. She takes the new members to one of the creepiest places where we have had activity and run through it at night, and I've got to tell you, some people haven't made it. They want nothing to do with us, and that's why we take them out there. You have to make sure they can perform in the field before you take them out on a real case."

Jim describes himself as a hard-core, science-based skeptic. Jim has been on some investigations, however, that made him question the validity of his beliefs. A case in point is an investigation the group did at an old school in Vermont. Legend has it that a janitor who passed away in the 1930s had been seen and heard in the school. "One of my guys went over there ahead of me," Jim said. "He was walking around doing EVP work, asking questions. One question he asked was 'Do you know that you're dead?' The spirit answered back, 'I'm still breathing.'" Jim returned to the school a few weeks later with a group from Vermont called VAPORS. "One of the girls and I had walked twenty feet down the hallway, and we noticed that the door to the bathroom was open," Jim said. "They had one of those infrared triggering devices on the wall panel near the inside of the door. So we checked the area between the door and whatever it was that set it off. We determined that you had to go a ways inside the bathroom to set it off. There was no way out of the bathroom, so whatever was triggering the motion detector was still in there." Jim and the young woman walked through the building to a different location where they could still see the room, and they asked the spirit to do it again, and the light came back on. Still, Jim is unwilling to cite this incident as definite proof of the paranormal because, after all, a motion detector is an electronic device and therefore is prone to malfunction. "It could be a coincidence too," Jim adds.

Ghosts are not the only paranormal entities that Jim hunts. "I've recently investigated some Bigfoot sightings," Jim says. "I went to Paris, Texas, on an expedition in April 2007, and we're going to Wisconsin later on to check up on a new creature. They describe it as a dog- or wolf-like Bigfoot creature, akin to what a werewolf would look like." Jim has never really been very interested in cryptozoology, but several of the members of his group are, so he started to investigate reports of strange creatures that have come to his attention. The prospect of hunting a creature like Bigfoot tantalizes Jim because the evidence might be more tangible than the evidence one collects while ghost hunting. "You might even be able to catch something physical. It's a lot more work than ghost hunting, though. While we were in Texas, we had wild pigs and tornadoes chasing us. We don't run into stuff like this in New England."

Jim Snell admits that not everyone becomes a paranormal investigator for the same reason. "Some have had a paranormal experience, and they want to figure it out, so they join a group," Jim says. "I don't think we will ever figure it all out, but I would like to experience enough of it firsthand to try to figure some of it out. Or at least to come up with my own theories that I can believe."

RHODE ISLAND

THE RHODE ISLAND PARANORMAL RESEARCH TEAM

Scituate, Rhode Island
Andrew Laird, Director
www.geocities.com/triprg/triprg.html

Andrew became involved in the field of paranormal research as the result of a bet between himself and his cofounder, Ray Lafaira: "I had been one of those people who liked to debunk the paranormal, so he and I made a bet. He would take me to a place, and if I didn't believe in ghosts after we went there, he would never bring up the subject again. We went up to an old asylum up in Massachusetts. He had already gotten permission to go in there. We spent about an hour and a half on the second floor of the Excitable Ward. I saw a man walk out of a room on the left-hand side of the hallway. He stopped and looked at me with Ray standing beside me. He then walked across the hall into another room. There was no way out of these rooms. These were cells. I walked up to the room where I saw the man walk in, and I said, 'Now, I've got you!' Ray just laughed. I walked into the room, and there was no one there. There was no way out of the room. I would have seen him if he had tried to get out. It was from that point on that I became fascinated with the paranormal." Andrew and Ray were unable to conduct a full-scale investigation of the place because it got to the point where it seemed as if everyone wanted to investigate it, and the authorities eventually stopped people from getting in.

Andrew and Ray started their group in September 1984. "We originally had four people, myself and three people I went to college with, and it grew from there. Right now, we have fourteen, and we are supposed to be interviewing three other people soon. We average about ten or eleven people," Andrew says. He describes the Rhode Island Paranormal Research Group as an "eclectic group and a half" that includes people from every religious background, including druids, wiccans, Christians, and Jews. "We're a total mix," Andrew says. "We all have something to add from our point of view on our investigations."

The group's mission is, in Andrew's words, "to bring the paranormal out of the dark that Hollywood has put it in. We want to prove that there is an afterlife, that there is something waiting for us on the other side. The proof that we present to people is pretty irrefutable that there is something on the other side." The Rhode Island Paranormal Research Group combines the metaphysical and the scientific approaches. Not only does the group employ an entire array of meters, computer software, and even closed-circuit TV, but it also relies on the abilities of four women and one man in the group who are psychics. "We confirm or don't confirm what the sensitives are getting, and they hit about eighty or ninety percent of the time," Andrew says. "They have picked out names that they could not have known before. Sometimes the psychics will guide us, and sometimes the people with the meters will guide the group. It depends on the place. Every place and every investigation is different."

The Rhode Island Paranormal Research Group does an equal number of historic sites and private homes. The group is currently conducting an ongoing investigation at the Penn House Museum, a seventeenth-century house in Covington, Rhode Island. "We've been investigating this place for two or three years. We're learning so much from the entities within this place. It's like when we did the Sprague Mansion in Cranston, Rhode Island. We investigated the Penn House Museum for two years," Andrew said. "And then there are other historic places that we will be in and out of in one night." He estimates that 90 percent of what the group finds in private residences is naturally occurring in the home. It has nothing to do with ghosts. Most of the time when the team debunks a haunting in a private home, the homeowners are relieved: "The first thing we tell them is, 'We don't think you're nuts, and we're here to find answers.' Sometimes they swear up and down that the place is haunted. After the investigation, we sit down with them and give them a full report. We don't just pack up our equipment and leave. We show them our findings, and it pleases them either way. As long as they know they're not losing their minds, they're happy, as a rule," Andrew says.

People find out about the Rhode Island Paranormal Research Group through the Internet and through interviews some of the members have done in magazines. The group has been featured on a number of television programs as well. One of their most publicized investigations was conducted at the *Charles W. Morgan*, a whaling ship in Mystic, Connecticut. "It was a media blitz," Andrew says. "It seems like every week we were on *Good Morning America* and 20/20, not to mention the local news." Some of the members have also served as consultants for the History Channel and the Discovery Channel. Still, Jason believes that the best way to promote his group is through word of mouth: "One person talks to another person. We have been around so long that people know us."

Andrew also believes that his group and others across the nation have benefited from the popularity of the *Ghost Hunters* television show. Andrew has tremendous respect for TAPS and the group's director: "I know Jason Hawes. I've met him a few times. He's a fine gentleman, but I've never worked with him. They have their ways of doing things, and we have our ways. We both come down to the same point. We are both trying to help people." Andrew admits, though, that people are often misled by what they see on television: "For the most part, the show has really opened the public to what we do. Every month, we interview two or three people who want to join the group, but when they find out that what we do has nothing to do with what they see in the movies, they change their minds. The reality of paranormal investigation has nothing to do with what you see television, TAPS included. Things could happen left and right, or you're bored out of your mind. The truth is that there's a lot of sitting and waiting."

Prospective members go through both a screening process and a six-month training period during which Andrew observes how they handle certain situations. "They work under the psychic team or the sensitive team," Andrew says. "They work under myself. We teach them how to use the equipment." In spite of the group's best efforts to screen and train new members, there have been many investigations where the group's members have been frightened. "You have to remember that we are dealing with the dead,"

Andrew says. "We might run into an entity that is not exactly friendly, and it lets you know that you're not welcome. Let's say the sensitives sit down and communicate with whatever entities might be in the area. At the same time, the safety person is in another part of the building, looking at monitors and listening to recordings. You might get an EVP that says, 'Get out of here!' I can think of four times when an investigator heard one of these EVPs and said, 'I'm leaving.'" Andrew believes that if too many investigators are in a single location, they can affect the entity with their negativity. They can make it stronger and allow it to break down any safety barriers the group has set up. Still, Andrew does not tell his members not to get scared. "It's good to get scared if you turn it into respect for what we're doing and for the entities we are dealing with," Andrew says.

Andrew finds it difficult to say which is his most memorable investigation because he learns something from every case. One of his favorites is the Penn House. "We have experienced almost all of the levels of paranormal activity in this place," Andrew said. "We've had hours and hours of EVP. We've had all kinds of videotape evidence. We haven't captured any full-body apparitions there, though. I wish we had." At the Sprague Mansion, the group was focusing its attention on the stairway, which is known to be haunted, when the members heard footsteps on the stairs and the landing. Several members immediately began taking photographs; one of them captured the image of a woman in a long gown walking up the stairway. They also caught the shadowy outline of a woman in a ball gown in the ballroom. "We have never caught something that looks exactly like a person," Andrew says. "That's the Holy Grail." At the Paine Mansion, the group photographed some orb activity. "On the video, you can tell by the way the dust moves when somebody walks through a room," Andrew says. "The dust is being moved by the breeze. All of a sudden, the dust is moving against the breeze and doing twists and turns. We caught a lot of that stuff, but we didn't catch any figures walking up the stairs or anything like that."

From Andrew's viewpoint, EVPs are much more significant than orbs because he is unable to prove that these tantalizing little spheres are paranormal: "I have played EVPs back for a client and heard her exclaim, 'Oh my God! That's my husband!' They recognize the voice. And it's an emotional high point for these people. Their skepticism just isn't there anymore. So we have no choice but to say this is real. This is about as real as it gets when you've got somebody who's not there talking to you." The group collected some very eerie EVPs at Saconawa Prison, which used to be a boys' reformatory. "We had a recording of Ray and Barbara setting up the equipment, but in the background, you can hear someone saying, 'Get out!' in a very ominous voice," Andrew said. At other locations, the groups have recorded similar threatening EVPs, such as "Get out of my house!" and "Get out and leave us alone!" Some of the language on the group's EVPs is so abusive that, in Andrew's words, it "would make a truck driver blush." The hostile tone of some of these EVPs can be traced, Andrew believes, to the fact that some of these spirits simply do not want to be bothered. Not all of the team's EVPs are angry, however. "We recorded one in the Paine House that is a little girl's voice," Andrew says. "Her name was Sarah. She told us to look in a particular place. We did, and we found a ring."

After the group has recorded EVPs, the members play them back for their clients. "We don't tell them what they are supposed to hear," Andrew says. "That would be like playing static and telling them they are supposed to be hearing 'The Pledge of Allegiance.' Before you know it, half of the people in the room would be hearing 'The Pledge of Allegiance.' We simply tell them, 'We recorded this. Tell us what you think.' " One EVP that the Rhode Island Paranormal Research Group recorded actually changed the life of one of its clients: "We got a call recently from a psychiatrist. His wife had just died. We set up at his house and stayed for a while. Then we decided to go back. When we decided to go back, we caught an EVP. We could hear his wife saying, 'You've go to let go.' She said this three different times at three different times of the night. The same voice. The same words. [The EVPs] were in the background of the doctor talking." After the group cleaned up the background noise of the EVP on the computer, the members played it back for the client, who was a hardened skeptic. Andrew said, "He heard it, his jaw dropped, and he said, 'Oh my God! That's Mary! But how can that be? She's right. I can't let go.' This was a doctor who taught psychology. He was the last person you would expect to say that he believed in ghosts. I am glad that I helped bring closure for the guy. It was definitely a positive experience for him." In Andrew's mind, this particular investigation was clearly a success because he and his team fulfilled the mission of the Rhode Island Paranormal Research: to bring closure to their clients at the same time that they are proving the existence of the paranormal.

NEW ENGLAND ANOMALIES RESEARCH
Warwick, Rhode Island
Keith Johnson, Director
www.nearparanormal.com

Keith Johnson is a tour guide in Pawtucket, Rhode Island. Before he founded New England Anomalies Research (NEAR) in 2004, he was a member of TAPS. "Carl [Keith's twin brother] and I were demonologists in the first season and part of the second season of the *Ghost Hunters* television show," Keith says. His present group started out with five members, but in three years, its membership has climbed to ninety. NEAR's members come from varied backgrounds, including a data processor, a bus driver, a clinical assistant, and an employee in an electronics firm. "My brother is a tour guide and into retail," Keith says. "My wife is a medical transcriptionist."

Even though Keith believes that everyone has psychic abilities, no one on Keith's team functions as a sensitive. "We have intuitions, and some of us, like myself, have enough discernment to be able to tell when there is something very, very negative in the atmosphere, but none of us are psychic," Keith says. For the most part, the members of NEAR employ the scientific method.

NEAR's mission is to explore the unknown and to document evidence as thoroughly as possible. "But we also want to help people, because a lot of our clients are scared and confused about what is going on," Keith says. "We are often called in to consult

with these people. We want to help people understand, and we
try to alleviate their fears so that they can deal with the problem."
NEAR's clients are particularly susceptible to fear because it is one
of the few groups in the country to specialize in negative situations. Keith says, "We are called in to all sorts of hauntings, but I
would say that forty to fifty percent of our investigations involve
the demonic. My wife and I do house cleansings, and it is because
we have that specialty that other groups call us in to assist as well.
We have worked closely with New England Paranormal, for example." If the evil entity is particularly insidious, Keith contacts members of the clergy. Often, however, ministers or priests turn Keith
down, either because they do not want to be involved with the
demonic or because they are not trained to handle these situations.
In that case, the members of NEAR have to deal with the demons
themselves.

The general public has been made aware of NEAR's specialization through the Internet. "We have a forum in our web site called
the Demonologist's Forum, whether people discuss the demonic and
every other aspect of paranormal investigation." Recent appearances on television shows have also raised the profile of NEAR.
"Besides *Ghost Hunters*, we have been on various newscasts and
have worked on documentaries as well. We will be in several of
the episodes of *Paranormal U.* on A & E in September." NEAR
also has its own public access television show in talk-show format.
"As far as I know, it is the first of its kind to deal with paranormal
investigation in a talk-show format," Keith says. NEAR's television
program also shows video clips of conferences the members have
attended, such as Penn State's UNICON in October 2006. "Also,
if we do a field trip investigation at a remote location, we will
show a fifteen- or twenty-minute clip of that," Keith says. Because
NEAR's reputation is so widespread, a workshop that Keith did at
Penn State was filled to capacity. "People were lined up down the
hallway for an hour waiting to get in. They had to be turned away
until the next day. That's how really popular [ghost hunting] is,"
Keith says. He admits that the public's response to NEAR's activities would probably have been more negative years ago, but now
people are more open to the possibility that there are spirits other

than human spirits out there. "I think the public in general has an interest in the unseen realm these days," Keith says.

In order to defend themselves against evil on their investigations, the members of NEAR supplement their audio and visual equipment with religious items. Keith says, "At times, we use blessed crosses or blessed water or blessed oil when we are using a house cleansing, where we pray in each room and anoint in each room. We also use scriptures to protect ourselves, because my wife and I are from a Christian background." Even though not all of the members of NEAR share the Johnsons' religious beliefs, Keith and his wife make sure that everyone is well protected when they are on a demonic case. Keith says that one can tell when a cleansing has been successful because the atmosphere is "lighter," much less oppressive. Before the group leaves the private residence, Keith tells the homeowners that it is now up to them to keep the demon from returning. "It might mean that the family members have to make certain changes in their lives, and they usually cooperate," Keith says. "For example, if someone has been using some sort of divination device like a Ouija board to contact spirits, we advise them to stop doing this because they are only drawing in more negativity. They are possibly opening a portal, and with that might come a lot of activity." From Keith's viewpoint, calling something that is unknown and unseen into one's house is just inviting trouble. Surprisingly, NEAR has not run into any serious conflicts with the religious community.

Most of the time, nothing really happens when NEAR is on-site. "It's a matter of taking data and reviewing it later," Keith says. "Once in a while, though, something will happen while you are there. Somebody will feel depressed. Somebody will be touched." Keith's wife Sandra, for example, has been touched twice on the top of her head. Fortunately, touching has been the extent of the group's physical contact with the spirits they have encountered. NEAR's clients, on the other hand, have not been so fortunate. "We were called in to do a private case in conjunction with TAPS. TAPS asked us to assist them because of the demonic implications. While we were there, scratches formed on the client's face," Keith said. "She was so overwhelmed by what was happening to her and her family that she just passed right out. Fortunately, we had a team member there who was familiar with first aid and had some medical training, so she stepped in and helped her out. The woman was so emotionally overwhelmed that she was hyperventilating." Keith said that this particular case was not filmed for the *Ghost Hunters* television show.

Not surprisingly, the fear factor can become a serious problem when investigating a site where the demonic might be involved. NEAR prepares its members for the unexpected even before they are accepted in the group. "We require that prospective members attend one of our classes so that they can really get a feel for what is going on," Keith says. "During the interview process, we explain that sometimes we do cases that involve the demonic. We also tell them that running away from a situation can be just as dangerous [as any ghost or demon]."

Even though NEAR considers itself a Christian group, clients who are not Christians are not turned away: "If they call us in, they have to accept that this is where we are coming from. We don't put down their religious beliefs. We tell them to focus on that which is positive instead of the negative. We tell them that if they are using a Ouija board to stop right away because that is probably making the situation worse." A client of New England Paranormal who leaned toward paganism has called NEAR in several times. "Even though we did a Christian blessing, she was very receptive because the wording I used was very conducive to her beliefs as far as positive energy and life-bringing forces are concerned. She found it very helpful and comforting," Keith says. NEAR actually prefers to investigate Christian homes because the members can proceed in their usual manner instead of trying to adapt their approach to coincide with the client's religious beliefs.

If NEAR is unable to detect the presence of spirits in a private residence, a few clients are disappointed. "We don't go away saying their house isn't haunted," Keith says. "We tell them we didn't find anything, but if they would like, we would certainly be willing to pray in each room and invite the positive spirits and positive energy. They are usually very conducive to that." As one would expect, a majority of NEAR's clients are very relieved when told that the group was unable to come up with an actual spirit.

H. P. Lovecraft, who was born in Providence, is, not surprisingly, an iconic figure among ghost hunters, paranormal enthusiasts, and horror fans in Rhode Island. Keith's brother Carl not only does a Lovecraft walking tour, but he also does an annual tribute to Lovecraft. He used to do them in the cemetery where Lovecraft is buried, but he now gives a lecture at Land Observatory because authorities no longer allow photography in the cemetery. This past year, about one hundred and thirty people turned out. During the Lovecraft celebration, fans do reenactments of Lovecraft's stories and read excerpts from his stories. Lovecraft's lasting appeal lies in the primary theme that permeates his work: that we are not as much in control as we think we are. "Fear is the strongest of emotions, and the greatest fear is of the unknown," Keith says. "That is what Lovecraft plays upon." For paranormal investigators who specialize in demonic hauntings, as NEAR does, fear is also a constant companion.

THE ATLANTIC PARANORMAL SOCIETY
Warwick, Rhode Island
Jason Hawes and Grant Wilson, Co-Directors
the-atlantic-paranormal-society.com

Jason Hawes founded his group after having a paranormal experience of his own, which he refuses to disclose. When he founded TAPS in 1990, it was originally called Rhode Island Paranormal. Jason and his fellow investigators began meeting in a local coffee shop. The group changed its name because it began handling cases within New England but outside of Rhode Island.[1] In order to gain the perspective of people with and without science backgrounds, Jason began recruiting people from a variety of professions, including nuclear physicists, police officers, computer programmers, and electrical engineers. In 1992, Grant Wilson, who was a web designer at the time, joined the group. He had had a paranormal experience four years after Jason's. Because TAPS tries to gain respectability by conducting investigations without charge, Jason and Grant have had to supplement their incomes by working as plumbers for Roto-Rooter. TAPS now has forty-four members in Rhode Island, Massachusetts, and Connecticut and forty-six bases in the United States and twelve other countries.[2] As a result of the popularity of the group's nationally broadcast television show *Ghost Hunters*, TAPS is the most high-profile paranormal research team operating in the United States today.

The primary mission of TAPS is to assist people who are experiencing disturbances in their homes that they suspect might be paranormal in origin. Jason and Grant believe that TAPS gives people who are experiencing fear and uncertainty in their own homes a place to turn to. The group routinely sends out teams consisting of three to six members to a client's residence. Using such scientific equipment as EMF detectors, tri-field meters, digital thermometers, thermal imagers, audio recorders, and infrared and digital cameras, TAPS usually spends between eight and twelve hours on an investigation.[3] Once the group's web site was set up, it began getting twenty thousand hits per day from all over the world.

The popularity of TAPS increased exponentially in 2004 when the Sci-Fi Channel approached Jason about doing a television show. "We received four offers for other shows before finally realizing that if we did not do this show and someone else did, how would they represent this field that we have put our hearts into? So that is why we are where we are today," Jason said. TAPS is exploiting the phenomenal success of its television show to help other paranormal groups. Paranormal research teams wishing to become a "TAPS Family Member" can put a link on their web sites to connect them to The Atlantic Paranormal Society's web page.

Today, TAPS has found outlets for disseminating information on the paranormal other than its television show and its web site. The group's monthly publication, *TAPS Paramagazine*, features articles on the paranormal and profiles of team members. In 2006, TAPS also began releasing podcasts, *TAPS Para-Radio*. In 2007, the name of *TAPS Para-Radio* was changed to *Beyond Reality*. It is now a live radio show broadcasting from WPRO in Rhode Island.

One research "tool" that Jason does not use very much in his group's investigations are psychics and mediums. "I believe in very few mediums," Jason says. "I think most of them have a 1-900 number attached to their name. Also, they always talk about how they were given this gift of sight, but I felt that if someone or something gave them a gift, it was not so they could charge people money to make themselves rich. I'd really like to get away from the sensitives who come in and do the floppy tuna, saying, 'Satan's living in your closet.'"[4]

In an interview published in *The New York Times*, Jason discussed the different types of spirits he and his group have encountered over the years. "The most benign are human hauntings," Jason said, "which divide into three types: intelligent spirits, which can converse with the living; residuals, which are leftover energies condemned to repeat one small action from their lives, like a recurring scene from a movie; and poltergeists, usually the spirits of young girls, which make a racket and can wreak havoc on property values." Human spirits, Jason says, can do very little damage because they can only lift about three to ten pounds. Human beings, on the other hand, can be very dangerous, and dealing with them requires the type of expertise and knowledge that the average group does not have.[5]

Unlike many groups that set out to prove that a site was haunted, TAPS has always tried to debunk the claims of the paranormal. "We at TAPS believe that over eighty percent of all cases that people believe to be paranormal activity are not," Jason says. By paranormal, Jason means, "above the normal." Grant says, "We go in, we listen to the stories, and with scientific research, we try to debunk the place. If we can't, then what is left is proof."[6] As a rule, TAPS tries to duplicate the phenomenon experienced by the homeowners. A typical case was one the group had in Winthrop, Massachusetts. A young couple, Jeff and Bekka Caruso, contacted TAPS regarding strange activity in their house. Bekka, who worked as a sales assistant for Knoll, said that she initially felt the presence of a white dog. Not long thereafter, the tranquillity of their home was disrupted by unexplained footsteps, doors slamming, and dressers emptying. The interviewer for the group was the first to sense that nothing paranormal was occurring in the house. After a few hours, the group determined that the Carusos' house was probably not haunted. However, to help ease the couple's fears, the group's demonologist, Keith Johnson, read a blessing on both floors of the house.[7]

Often, the origins of the disturbances in people's homes are very mundane. For example, a couple informed TAPS that the ghost of their dead uncle was flushing their toilet every night at two A.M. Using their plumber skills, Jason and Grant quickly determined that the flapper valve on the toilet was leaking slightly. "For about three hours into the night, the water would be down just to where—KA-CHEE—it'd start running again."[8] On another case, a little girl woke up every night screaming because someone—or something—was poking her. TAPS set up a video camera in the child's room and discovered that her brother, who slept in the bunk above, jabbed her every night and then pretended to be asleep.[9]

However, not every haunting can be easily explained away. At Eastern State Penitentiary, a video camera captured the image of a black-caped figure swooping down the hallway. During an episode of *Ghost Hunters* that was filmed at a National Guard armory in New Bedford, Massachusetts, a sound technician was knocked flat on his back. Video footage clearly showed his forty-pound equipment bag, which was attached to his waist, flying up and hitting him in the face.[10] In October 2005, TAPS conducted an investigation at the Moon River Brew Pub in Savannah, Georgia. After the pub closed at eleven-thirty, the group set up its audio and visual equipment, turned off the lights, and went to work. One of the video cameras captured a small ball of light flying across the room. A close examination of the tape revealed the light anomaly to be nothing more than a flying insect. However, at midnight, the TAPS members collected some evidence that could not be easily explained. While walking through the basement with a thermal imager, they captured a blue blob of light that appeared to be a human shape. The investigators also detected a ten-degree drop in temperature at the exact location where the entity was seen. TAPS feels that corroborating evidence like this is much more convincing that a single, isolated anomaly.[11]

Because ghost hunting and technology go hand in hand these days, any significant improvement in the equipment investigators use will have a positive impact on the field. On October 31, 2006, viewers of the *Ghost Hunters* television show were able to participate in a six-hour investigation of the Stanley Hotel in Estes Park, Colorado, via an on-line video feed. People watching the investigation at home were able to send suggestions and comments to the show's producers while sitting at the computer. The added star power of CM Punk of Extreme Championship Wrestling turned the investigation into a major media event for the Sci-Fi Channel.[12]

Humor, both intentional and unintentional, has certainly enhanced the appeal of *Ghost Hunters*. Jason is aware of the pitfalls of taking oneself—or one's interests—too seriously. For example, several years ago, TAPS was invited to investigate a private residence. Midway through one investigation, the elderly lady who lived in the house forgot who they were and chased the team out of her house with a frying pan. "The living frighten me far more than the dead," Jason says.[13]

VERMONT

PARANORMAL INVESTIGATORS
OF NEW ENGLAND
South Burlington, Vermont
Jeffrey Stewart
www.pinewengland.com

Jeffrey Stewart did not really think much about the spirit world until he began working as a private investigator. "I ran into a case where someone claimed to have paranormal activity," Jeffrey said, "and I thought, 'Well, that's a little odd. I've never had that kind of case before.' In 2001, I contacted this group in Massachusetts, Orion Paranormal, and I instantly got hooked." Jeffrey was trained by the director of the group, who is a parapsychologist. "After that, I joined Ghost Investigations.Com. They decided to fall apart, and about two years ago, I decided to start a group on my own," Jeffrey said.

Jeffrey founded Paranormal Investigators of New England in 2004. "We train our investigators OJT—on-the-job training," Jeffrey said. "We tell them to try to keep an open mind and a skeptical mind at the same time. We train them one by one on different equipment until they know it by heart. Everybody knows their roles and takes turns on the equipment." Most of his members hold day jobs in the professions. "I'm an engineer," Jeffrey said. "We have a psychologist who is in college studying to be a parapsychologist. He is also a full-time child advocate. We also have a professional photographer who is a photographic analyst. We have an engineer like myself and a machinist. The photographer can debunk some of the anomalies people capture on film. The psychologist can get a better idea of people and how their lives work and whether or not there is genuine paranormal activity. My experience as a private investigator has helped me with my surveillance capabilities. I can tell where to set up, and I bring a lot of technical knowledge to our investigations." On most investigations, the members work in teams of two or three. "We never have anyone alone, not only in case something happens, but you always want a witness in case you were unable to capture something on video or still camera," Jeffrey says. Even though Paranormal Investigators of New England is independent, its members work closely with another group in Vermont.

When the group investigates depends on the clients' needs. "There's no difference from night or day except that during the day, if a car passes by, you can see fifteen different reflections through the windows as opposed to one reflection from a headlight. It's easier to investigate at night because the equipment we have is strictly night vision," Jeffrey says.

Most of the group's cases are private residences. The members screen all of their clients before they accept a case. "We'll go down and interview them and one or two of us try get a feel of the place," Jeffrey says. "We also do a preliminary investigation. We try to do a little history research too." Jeffrey feels that he can get a general sense of people's character in the interviewing process: " You don't really know what the person's going to tell you. They could be extremely 'out there,' or they could be telling you the truth about what they've seen." The group also asks clients about their religious beliefs. "We don't want to step on any local religion's toes, so to speak," Jeffrey says. He believes the group has had no conflicts with the religious community because the members take such great care not to offend anyone.

The fact that the group is 100 percent science-based could also explain why the group has been accepted by the general public. "We don't use sensitives or mediums or clergy or anyone with a religious background," Jeffrey says. Still, he has not ruled out the possibility that some people really do possess psychic abilities: "I did security for a long time before getting into engineering. Being in a dark, creepy building, you sometimes get a sense of not quite being alone, and then you find the homeless man underneath the stairs. When you get the feeling that you are being watched, that might be a sixth sense."

Clients find out about Paranormal Investigators of New England through the Internet and word of mouth. The group's investigations have also been reported in the local newspaper and television stations. Paranormal Investigators of New England has also benefited from its relations with a local author, Joseph Citro, who has promoted the group in public appearances.

The mission of Paranormal Investigators of New England is to find the truth in any scenario, whether it is paranormal activity or not. "We are here to help, like most groups are," Jeffrey says. "We are skeptical; we investigate with an open mind. We keep tabs on our investigation, whether it leans toward the paranormal or there are domestic issues, like if the floor creaks." Unlike many groups, Paranormal Investigators of New England does not visit a site with the intention of proving the existence of the paranormal by the end of the investigation. "Like most researchers, you have to be skeptical because no one has the answer, and there is no proof of the phenomenon," Jeffrey says. "In fact, only three percent of all the cases I have had over the last eight years were actually haunted." Approximately 50 percent of the group's clients are pleased when told that there is no paranormal activity in their house. "A lot of people today, they want to believe that their place is haunted," Jeffrey says. "To me, it doesn't matter if I debunk a haunting or not because my main focus is to help people in need, so if they're disappointed, we tell them that from what we hear, having a ghost in your house is not necessarily a good thing. It's kind of a hype nowadays, but from what we understand, it can turn for the worse as well. I think TAPS is partially responsible for this, but it's not their fault. They've been together a long time, and they are very professional."

Paranormal Investigators of New England collects evidence using most of the standard scientific equipment: infrared cameras, Hi8, minicams, digital and thirty-five-millimeter still cameras, and EMF detectors. The group also carries around ambient thermometers. Because the group does not charge for its investigations, most of the members buy their own equipment. The group does not have an office yet, so the members process the evidence individually. Jeffrey embarks on every investigation hoping to photograph a full-body apparition. "Several members have seen them, and for some of them, that's the reason why they joined the group," Jeffrey says. The most significant evidence the group has collected so far is EVPs.

One of the best EVPs was collected at St. Albans Bible Street School in St. Albans, Vermont. "We started investigating there eight years ago and have returned many times," Jeffrey says. "One of the questions I asked was 'Do you know you're dead?' because I try to go for the shock factor. When I analyzed the evidence, I heard a slow voice stating, 'I'm still breathing.' I am a skeptic, and just hearing that almost direct answer to my question caught me off guard. This put me in a difficult position as a skeptic because it is so convincing." Because EVPs are so convincing, some of Jeffrey's clients do not want to hear them because they do not want to believe their house to be haunted. As mind-numbing as EVPs can be, Jeffrey does not accept them by themselves as proof that ghosts are present. "I do try to get collaborative evidence," Jeffrey says. "Let's say we get an 2.0 spike on the EMF detector and we got an EVP in the same room, we'll write that down in the report and reveal that to our clients."

So far, the group has only had two demonic cases. In both investigations, the members were unable to prove scientifically that the homeowners had anything there, demonic or any other type of entity. "They still claim to this day that the demons are there," Jeffrey said. "We told them to contact religious organizations to get them to bless the house because that has been proven to work in the past. Because there is no way to prove the existence of angels or demons, then there's no way to do the research to learn how to get rid of them, except to tell them to leave."

Jeffrey has been involved in a number of great investigations, but the most memorable was a little bed-and-breakfast in St. Albans, Vermont. The group did not get any really significant scientific evidence, but the group had an abundance of personal experiences. "We had the place to ourselves. We went to bed at three A.M. because we had stayed up all night investigating," Jeffrey said. "We just left the cameras rolling. We heard voices out in the hall, but because of our exhaustion, we figured it was some of the other investigators. It turned out it wasn't anybody. We felt pretty foolish because our camera wasn't even on the location where we heard the voices and footsteps. We couldn't tune in to what was said, but it still caught our attention."

Although no members of Jeffrey's group have been physically frightened, one of the members did have a very odd dream about one of the places they were investigating. "We went back and did research and found out that her dream was very close to what had happened," Jeffrey said. "We usually just try to find out the age and era of the property and then find out the rest of the information afterwards. She said she had a very lifelike dream of a crying little girl in this room. The dream was very emotional for her. She woke up in tears. After we did the investigation, we did research and found out that a little girl did die in the building. Apparently, she was abused. It struck her [the member] pretty hard."

Jeffrey disagrees with those groups that believe that cemeteries are good training grounds for new members: "I've only done three cemeteries, and that's only because they had the reputation of being haunted. If they're dead, the last thing they'd want to be around is their corpse. If I were dead, I wouldn't want to watch my body rot in the grave. When we pass on, what people are seeing is an imprint of energy on time and space. That's more believable than an intelligent haunting, a ghost knowing what people are doing. It is more likely that ghosts are disembodied energy floating through time and space. That is a residual haunting. Residual hauntings are on a certain time and a certain date, you're going to see the apparition. If Grandpa got up to smoke his pipe at one A.M., you are probably going to see him smoke his pipe at one A.M. as a residual haunting."

In recent years, Paranormal Investigators of New England has not confined its investigations exclusively to hauntings. The group also looks into reports of Bigfoot activity, UFOs, and "Champ," Lake Champlain's legendary lake monster. "So we are true paranormal investigators—we investigate all aspects of the paranormal," Jeffrey says.

VERMONT AGENCY OF PARANORMAL RESEARCH (VAPOR)

Swanton, Vermont
Monica Robayo and Anthony Chaput, Co-Directors
www.teamvapor.org

One can honestly say that Monica Robayo has been investigating the paranormal for most of her life. "When I was a little kid, I'd go up into the attic and turn the lights out to see if there was a ghost. After *Ghost Hunters* on the Sci-Fi Channel started the ghost-hunting craze, I realized that there are lots of people out there like me who do this, not for a living, but as a hobby," Monica says. She wanted to join a paranormal research group that was already established, but the closest one was in Maine, so she came up with a name and started her own group. The nucleus of the group became members of her own family—her father, her brother, her sister-in-law, and her partner—all of whom were passionate about ghost hunting. The eight-member group now includes the manager of a seafood restaurant, a stay-at-home mom, a truck driver, a web designer, and a volunteer. Monica is a receptionist at a local pool company. VAPOR's mission is to figure out why one place becomes haunted as opposed to another place. The group also wants to help homeowners understand why these disturbances are occurring at their home.

VAPOR is primarily science-based, but the group does take advantage of one of their member's psychic abilities on occasion. Team member Anthony Chaput says, "We use her as a tool. If she feels that a place has spirits, we make note of it. If she feels that there's something standing at a certain spot, we'll take more pictures. We usually team her up with somebody else."

Before new members are permitted to participate in an investigation, Monica has a serious talk with them about what to do in "scary" situations: "We tell them if something [spooky] occurs, walk toward it. If you're scared, just call out in a normal tone to your partner." Monica is proud of the fact that so far, none of her members have been visibly frightened on an investigation. Most of them, in fact, are looking forward to seeing a ghost. "They're all looking forward to experiencing something. We all want that magical moment when a full-bodied apparition says, 'Hello.'"

Monica's group has a very clear-cut strategy for publicizing the group. "During Halloween, we contact the local radio station to get our name out there," Monica says. "We arrange to have articles written about us in the local newspaper in October as well." To garner publicity during the "off-season," Monica has had to "think outside the box": "We've been thinking of contacting real estate companies. Maybe if they know about us, they will grant us access to certain locations." Even though Monica believes that the *Ghost Hunters* television show depends too much on editing, she has to admit that becoming a member of the TAPS family has really increased the group's case load: "The show has definitely gotten the word out. Ever since we've joined the TAPS family, we have received more recognition."

Monica believes that the interview process is a crucial element of any successful investigation: "The main question we ask homeowners in the interview process is, 'What do you expect to get out of this?'" After talking to one owner, the group realized that the house was most likely harboring a demonic entity. "We let them know that we couldn't get rid of it," Monica said, "but we told them that we could help *them* find a way to get rid of it. We were very careful to work with their religious beliefs." At the time of this interview, Monica was trying to recruit clergy to assist the group with cleansings or exorcisms.

The desire to believe too much in the paranormal can really compromise an investigation. Monica prefers to pair up a skeptic with a believer to enhance the credibility of the evidence they collect. Problems also occur when clients really want to be told that a ghost was responsible for the activity in their home. Monica says, "We try to figure out the logical cause first. If a family hears voices, we'll ask, 'What kind of duct work does the house have?' The voices might be carried from one room to the next through the duct work." Sometimes, telling a client that ghosts are not involved can be heartbreaking, especially if the ghost is reputed to be the spirit of a loved one. For example, a mother who had lost her son went to the cemetery and took a photograph over his grave. After she developed the film, she was certain that she had captured the spectral image of her son. She contacted a couple of paranormal groups and was told that she had photographed a tombstone. Seeking a third opinion, she enlarged the photograph and brought it to VAPOR. "It looks like there's a transparent human figure standing in the background," Anthony said. "Three of us went out to the cemetery, and it took us between thirty and forty-five minutes to find the exact place where the woman was standing when she took the picture. I placed one of my members, Robert, in the exact place where he was standing next to the tree. We took a couple of photos and discovered that the woman's 'ghost' was actually fifteen tombstones lined up together to make one perfect, humanoid figure." Understandably, the woman was disappointed when Monica held up the group's photograph against her photograph and proved that she was mistaken. She did, however, tell her to keep her photograph and to post it on her web site.

Like the best paranormal research groups, VAPOR is very critical of the evidence its members collect on an investigation. EMF detectors are not totally reliable because they can be affected by wiring in a house. Monica will accept an orb as evidence only if it is, in her words, "spectacular." EVPs are more convincing than orbs, but they can also be problematic "If you think a voice said 'Good-bye,' then every time you hear it, you'll hear 'Good-bye,'" Monica said. "That's just how the mind works. When someone does capture an EVP, we'll play it for the client without telling what we have heard so that we can get their unbiased view on it." The best EVPs, Monica believes, consist of actual syllables and words. They are crystal clear.

EVPs played a prominent role in one of the group's most fascinating investigations. VAPOR was investigating a local bed-and-breakfast that was rumored to be haunted. Legend has it that the bed-and-breakfast is haunted by a female spirit. "We had the entire property to ourselves that night," Monica said. "We were on the first floor getting ready to begin our investigation. A few minutes later, we checked a video camera that we had set up on the third floor, and we clearly heard a giggle. There is no way our voices could have carried that far." Toward the end of the investigation, Monica and Anthony were walking down the staircase. After Anthony reached the bottom of the stairs, he checked his digital voice recorder, which had been running the entire time, and was startled to hear what he described as a "strained scream." Later, the group discovered that two digital voice recorders on the third floor and one recorder in the attic had captured the same strained scream.

So far, VAPOR has not run into any conflict with the religious community, except for Monica's mother. "My mother says, 'Leave the dead alone!' She's pretty religious. She doesn't even want to discuss [ghost hunting] with me," Monica says. Anthony is certain that Monica's mother is in the minority. "We were on the front page of the local newspaper on Halloween, and we didn't get any negative reactions," Anthony said.

The Ghost Hunter's Toolbox

Barometer Some investigators believe that entities can affect barometric pressure, so a barometer could be used to verify readings from other types of equipment.

Batteries Parapsychologists theorize that spirits must draw from surrounding energy sources in order to manifest themselves. Bringing along extra batteries is a good idea in case batteries in cameras or meters are drained.

Cameras Most investigators prefer thirty-five-millimeter SLR cameras over digital cameras, which can create false orbs through light refractions and "defect" pixels.

Candles and matches Candles can come in very handy if the flashlight batteries are drained, a common occurrence on paranormal investigations.

Compass Not only will a compass help investigators orient themselves in unfamiliar surroundings, but it can also pick up electromagnetic forces.

Dowsing rods Fashioned out of wire, like coat hangers, dowsing rods are said to be sensitive to electromagnetic fields. Dowsing rods can also be purchased. They are favored mostly by metaphysical groups.

EMF detectors These hand-held meters measure fluctuations in the electromagnetic field.

Flashlights Flashlights are indispensable in a building after it has "gone dark" or in a cemetery at night.

Geiger counters These devices measure fluctuations in radiation, which could point to a disturbance in spirit energy.

First aid kit Band-Aids and disinfectant can come in very handy on those dark nights when it is easy to trip over a tombstone or a fallen limb.

Headset communicators Many investigators prefer these devices over walkie-talkies because the user's hands are free to do other things while talking.

Infrared thermal scanner Infrared thermal scanners have the ability to detect cold spots. They are particularly useful outdoors.

Ion counter　Some investigators bring along ion counters because of the belief that spirits generate large numbers of positive ions.

Infrared thermometers　Noncontact thermometers measure temperature at a distance and therefore do not have to be moved from one cold spot to another.

Motion detectors　These are ideal for sensing movement in a room or hallway.

Night-vision scope　This device allows the investigator to see in the dark without an external light source. It can also enable the user to see into the infrared realm.

Notebook and pencil　Many investigators take note of the time and type of paranormal activity occurring during an investigation.

Plastic bags　Small, lunch-sized bags can be used for collecting material evidence at a site.

Spotlights　Small, battery-powered swivel spotlights that sit on the ground come in handy when setting up or dismantling equipment.

Talcum powder　Talcum powder can be used to capture footprints or handprints during an investigation.

Tri-field meter　This meter combines magnetic and electric readings.

Video cameras　Video cameras not only capture events that are happening, like moving orbs, but they have also been known to pick up EVPs.

Voice recorder　Digital recorders are rapidly replacing conventional tape recorders as the best device for recording EVPs. Tape recorders should have an external static-free microphone.

Walkie-talkies　Walkie-talkies can be very useful when a group is investigating a large area.

Watch　Watches are essential for recording the exact time when a paranormal event occurs.

Notes

Introduction (pages ix–xv)

1. Richmond Beatty, *The American Tradition in Literature*, 3rd ed., vol. 1 (New York: W. W. Norton, 1967), 5.
2. Marilynne Roach, *The Salem Witch Trials; A Day-by-Day Chronicle of a Community Under Siege* (New York: Taylor Trade Publishing, 2004), 76.
3. Cotton Mather, *The Wonders of the Invisible World* (1693), reprinted in *The Literature of the United States*, ed. Walter Blair (Chicago: Scott, Foresman and Company, 1966), 142.
4. Cheri Revai, *Haunted Massachusetts* (Mechanicsburg, Penn.: Stackpole Books, 2005), 23.
5. Cheri Revai, *Haunted Connecticut* (Mechanicsburg, Penn.: Stackpole Books, 2006), 7.
6. Charles A. Stansfield, *Haunted Vermont* (Mechanicsburg, Penn.: Stackpole Books, 2007), 39.
7. Charles Stansfield, *Haunted Maine* (Mechanicsburg, Penn.: Stackpole Books, 2007), 18.
8. Thomas D'Agostino, *Haunted New Hampshire* (Atglen, Penn.: Schiffer, 2007), 88.
9. Thomas D'Agostino, *Haunted Rhode Island* (Atglen, Penn.: Schiffer, 2005), 76.
10. Troy Taylor, *Ghosts by Gaslight* (Decatur, Ill.: Whitechapel Press, 2007), 22.
11. Ibid., 46.
12. Ibid., 36.
13. Ibid., 70.
14. Deborah Blum, *Ghost Hunters: William James and the Search for Scientific Proof of Life after Death* (New York: Penguin Press, 2006), 86.
15. Daniel Hoffman, *Poe Poe Poe Poe Poe Poe Poe* (New York: Avon Books, 1972), 28.
16. *Mobil Travel Guide Road Atlas* (New York: GeoNova Publishing, 2007), 247, 242, 236, 255, 250, 258.

Rhode Island (pages 134–38)

1. Jill M. Rohrbach, "Eureka Springs to be featured on Sci-Fi Channel's Ghost Hunters episode." *Arkansas Media Room*. Published 22 July 2005. Retrieved 5 July 2007. http://www.arkansasmediaroom.com/news-releases/listings/display.asp?id=662.

2. "Interview with Jason Hawes—31st July 2005." *Bad Psychics*. Retrieved 6 July 2007. http://badpsychics.com/thefraudfiles.modules/sections/index.php?op=viewarticle&artid=37.

3. John Leland, "Don't say ghostbuster, Say spirit plumber," *New York Times*. Published 31 October 2002. Retrieved 19 April 2007. http://the-atlantic-paranormal-society.com/inthemedia/nytimes.html.

4. Russ Bynum. "TV Ghost Hunters tackle America's 'most haunted' city." Published 10 October 2005. Retrieved 5 July 2007. http://media.www.dailygamecock.com/media/storage/paper247/news/2005/10/10/News/Tv.Ghost.Hunters.Tackle.Americas.most.Haunted.City-1015309.shtml

5. Leland, *op. cit.*

6. Jessica Clark. "'Ghost Hunters' tape episode in St. Augustine." *First Coast News*. Published 17 January 2006. Retrieved 5 July 2007. http://wwww.firstcoastnews.com/news/local/news-article.aspx?storyid=50099.

7. Leland, *op. cit.*

8. Bynum, *op. cit.*

9. Rohrbach, *op. cit.*

10. Bynum, *op. cit.*

11. Bynum, *op. cit.*

12. Jon Donnis. "'Ghost Hunters' (TAPS): Sci-Fi Channel in America ran a special Ghost Hunters Live show just for Halloween." *Bad Psychics*. Published 2 November 2006. Retrieved 6 July 2007. http://badpsychics.com/thefraudfiles/modules/news/article.php?storyid-236.

13. Andy Smith, "Ghost Hunters on the job this Halloween," *Rhode Island News*. Published 30 October 2006. Retrieved 5 July 2007. http://www.projo.com/tv/content/projo-20061020-ghosthunters30.8c99c540.html.

Filmography

Movies Dealing With Paranormal Investigations and Exorcisms

The Amityville Horror (1979). Directed by Stuart Rosenberg. Starring James Brolin, Margot Kidder, Rod Steiger, Don Stroud, and Murray Hamilton.
Based on Jay Anson's book about George and Kathy Lutz, who move into a Long Island home where Ronald DeFeo, Jr., murdered his entire family, this cliché-ridden film is truly frightening only when it deals with real-life horrors, like misplacing large sums of money. Rod Steiger's hammy performance as a priest who attempts to bless the house is an entertaining distraction. The musical score, which resembles a demented lullaby, is a horror classic.

The Amityville Horror (2005). Directed by Andrew Douglas. Starring Ryan Reynolds and Melissa George.
This remake of the 1979 film adaptation of Jay Anson's book makes drastic revisions in the original movie script, such as making George Lutz a homicidal maniac and adding the ghost of one of the children murdered by Ronald DeFeo, Jr. The film has clearly been "re-envisioned" for modern audiences nurtured on fast-paced editing, gore, and very buff male physiques.

Dominion: Prequel to the Exorcist (2005). Directed by Paul Schraeder. Starring Stellen Skarsgard, Gabriel Mann, Clara Bellar, and Billy Crawford.
Set in the late 1940s, this film focuses on Father Merrin, who is drawn to Africa by the discovery of an ancient church buried in the desert. Merrin does battle with his personal demons and with the demon Pazuzu. The studio scrapped this prequel to *The Exorcist* on the grounds that its horror quotient was too low. Beautifully photographed by Vittorio Storaro, this thinking man's thriller is marred by a disappointingly flat climax.

The Entity (1983). Directed by Sidney J. Furie. Starring Barbara Hershey and Ron Silver.
Parapsychologists come to the aid of a woman claiming she has been beaten and raped by a ghost. Supposedly based on Carlotta Morgan's actual experiences, this sensationalistic movie forfeits credibility in the end when the parapsychologists "capture" the entity.

The Exorcism of Emily Rose (2005). Directed by Scott Derrickson. Starring Laura Linney, Tom Wilkinson, and Campbell Scott.
True story of a priest who is accused of murder after a teenage girl dies during an exorcism. This courtroom drama is well directed and acted, but it lacks the energy of *The Exorcist* because it dwells on the legal and ethics issues in the case.

The Exorcist (1973). Directed by William Friedkin. Starring Ellen Burstyn, Max von Sydow, Jason Miller, Kitty Winn, Lee J. Cobb, and Linda Blair.
This blockbuster thriller is very loosely based on a true story about a twelve-year-old girl who is possessed by a demon. *The Exorcist*, which is based on William Peter Blatty's best-selling novel, is not only one of the most frightening films ever made, but it is generally considered to be a fairly accurate depiction of an actual exorcism.

Exorcist II: The Heretic (1977). Directed by John Boorman. Starring Richard Burton, Linda Blair, Louise Fletcher, Kitty Winn, and James Earl Jones.
A priest tries to cast out the demon that is still living inside teenager Regan MacNeil. The African subplot does little to advance the plot of this muddled thriller. A tremendous disappointment from a talented director.

The Exorcist III (1990). Directed by William Peter Blatty. Starring George C. Scott, Brad Dourif, Jason Miller, Nicol Williamson, Scott Wilson, and Ed Flanders.
Police inspector Bill Kinderman investigates a string of gruesome murders connected to Regan MacNeil's 1973 exorcism. The film has a promising beginning, but the ending is confusing and seems rushed.

Exorcist—The Beginning (2004). Directed by Renny Harlin. Starring Stellaen Skarsgård, Izabella Scorupco, James D'Arcy, and Julian Wadham.
This second version of Father Merrin's trip to East Africa in 1949 to investigate a recently discovered church buried in the sand for almost

two millennia is a straightforward, action-packed thriller. *Exorcist—The Beginning* is definitely more exciting than Paul Schraeder's version, but not nearly as thought-provoking.

1408 (2007). Directed by Mike Håfström. Starring John Cusak and Samuel L. Jackson.
The author of true-haunting books like *Ten Nights in Haunted Hotel Rooms* receives a postcard warning him not to spend the night in room 1408 of the Dolphin Hotel. Based on a short story by Stephen King, this scarefest will resonate with ghost hunters, many of whom have investigated haunted hotels themselves, albeit with less spectacular results. *1408* is definitely one of the best film adaptations of a work by Stephen King.

Ghostbusters (1984). Directed by Ivan Reitman. Starring Bill Murray, Dan Aykroyd, Harold Ramis, Sigourney Weaver, Rick Moranis, Annie Potts, and Ernie Hudson.
Three paranormal investigators set up shop in New York City and build a thriving business rounding up the "Big Apple's" rampant spirits. This blockbuster comedy scores high on laughs, but it also created a laughable image of ghost hunters that exists to this day. On the other hand, the film could be said to target people who take themselves too seriously, a charge that applies to many people working in the field of paranormal research.

Ghostbusters II (1989). Directed by Ivan Reitman. Starring Bill Murray, Dan Aykroyd, Sigourney Weaver, Harold Ramis, Rick Moranis, Ernie Hudson, and Peter MacNicol.
This over-long sequel brings the trio of ghost hunters back to New York City after a five-year hiatus to stave off another "slime attack" from the other side. The now-familiar story benefits from eyepopping special effects and from a scene-stealing performance by Peter MacNicol.

The Haunted (1991). Directed by Robert Mandel. Starring Sally Kirkland, Jeffrey DeMunn, Louise Latham, Joyce Van Patton, Stephen Markle, Diane Baker, and George D. Wallace.
A Catholic family moves into an old Pennsylvania home, find that it is haunted, and seeks help from priests, paranormal researchers, and the media. The made-for-television movie, based on the book written by Robert Curran, is a very well-handled treatment of the Smurl family's battles with demons, the media, and disbelieving neighbors.

The Haunting (1963). Directed by Robert Wise. Starring Julie Harris, Richard Johnson, Claire Bloom, and Russ Tamblyn.

A college professor, two psychics, and a young heir spend the night in a ninety-year-old haunted house in New England. This harrowing film, based on the Shirley Jackson novel *The Haunting of Hill House*, creates terror and suspense totally through lighting and eerie sound effects. *The Haunting* is still considered one of the greatest horror films ever made.

The Haunting (1999). Directed by Jan De Boot. Starring Liam Neeson, Catherine Zeta Jones, Owen Wilson, Lili Taylor, Virginia Madsen, and Bruce Dern.

This boring remake of the 1963 horror classic tries unsuccessfully to generate thrills through elaborate computer-generated imagery (CGI) effects. The revised plot involving the wealthy owner of a nineteenth-century textile mill who exploits children does not improve on Shirley Jackson's novel.

The Legend of Hell House (1973). Directed by John Hough. Starring Roddy McDowell, Pamela Franklin, Clive Revill, and Peter Bowles.

A psychic, a psychiatrist and his wife, and the only survivor of a previous investigation spend the night in a haunted mansion. Based on the Richard Matheson novel by the same name, this thrilling haunted-house movie boasts an intelligent script and a talented cast. Like the best horror movies, *The Legend of Hell House* generates chills without relying on excessive gore.

Near Death (2003). Directed by Joe Castro. Starring Perrine Moore, Scott Lunsford, and Ali Willingham.

Three paranormal researchers investigate the home of a deceased B-movie director and encounter a pack of ghouls. This ultra-cheap film boasts impressive computer effects buts suffers from a poor script and amateurish acting.

Poltergeist (1982). Directed by Tobe Hooper. Starring Craig T. Nelson, JoBeth Williams, Heather O'Rourke, Beatrice Straight, Zelda Rubinstein, and Dominique Dunne.

The five-year-old daughter of a couple living in a suburban tract home is kidnapped by ghosts and transported to another dimension. Producer Steven Spielberg's box-office smash starts out slowly but builds to a riveting climax. This is one of the first major studio productions to feature a somewhat science-based paranormal investigation. Top-rate special effects are still effective today. The deaths of Heather O'Rourke and Dominique Dunne fueled speculation that the film and its sequels were cursed.

Poltergeist II (1986). Directed by Brian Bigson. Starring Craig T. Nelson, JoBeth Williams, Heather O'Rourke, Will Sampson, Oliver Rubins, and Zelda Rubinstein.
A Native American shaman comes to the aid of the Freeling family, who are terrorized by the unquiet spirits of a nineteenth-century religious cult. This meaningless sequel is saved by its likable cast and some spectacular special effects.

Poltergeist III (1988). Directed by Gary Sherman. Starring Tom Skerritt, Nancy Allen, Heather O'Rourke, Zelda Rubinstein, and Lara Flynn Boyle.
Carol Anne moves in with her aunt and uncle and is still beset by otherworldly forces. Moving the setting from the suburbs to the big city is the only difference between this predictable film and its two predecessors.

Rose Red (2002). Directed by Craig R. Baxley. Starring Nancy Travis, Matt Keslar, Kimberly J. Brown, and David Dukes.
A group of people with psychic powers spend the night in a haunted mansion under the supervision of a psychology professor. This television mini-series, penned by Stephen King, borrows heavily from *The Haunting* and the legends surrounding the Winchester House. This familiar story is enlivened by a cast of colorfully eccentric characters.

Sightings: Heartland Ghost (2007). Directed by Brian Trenchard-Smith. Starring Beau Bridges, Nia Long, Miguel Ferrer, Gabriel Olds, and Thea Gill.
A group of paranormal investigators visit a Midwestern home in which the husband has been physically attacked by the ghost of a little girl named Sallie. The dramatization of an actual haunting featured in the *Sightings* television series, this made-for-television movie embellishes the actual incident without distorting the facts to an appreciable extent.

The St. Francisville Experiment (1995). Directed by Ted Nicholaou. Starring Ryan Larson, Dan Scanlan, Madison Charas, Paul Palmer, and Tim Baldini.
Four young filmmakers attempt to investigate and cleanse an antebellum home in St. Francisville, Louisiana, where the infamous Madame

LaLaurie is reputed to have fled after being chased out of New Orleans by a mob. This blatant rip-off of *The Blair Witch Project* benefits from on-location filming and a brief appearance by the president of the American Ghost Society, Troy Taylor. Ironically, the film's low budget enhances the sense of verisimilitude.

White Noise (2005). **Directed by Geoffrey Sax. Starring Michael Keaton, Chandra West, and Ian McNeice.**
After an architect's wife dies in a tragic accident, he becomes obsessed with interpreting messages from her embedded in the white noise found on television and radio. The first commercial movie whose plot focuses on electronic voice phenomena (EVPs), *White Noise* engages the viewer with its instructive explanation of paranormal science, but it eventually turns into a conventional thriller.

Index

133.10974 B877   INFCW
Brown, Alan,
Ghost hunters of New England /

CENTRAL LIBRARY
12/10